# finding
# FAMILY

# finding FAMILY

## How Deeply Rooted Faith Grew Our Family Tree

### WENDY BATCHELDER

REDEMPTION PRESS

Published by Redemption Press, PO Box 427, Enumclaw, WA 98022.

Toll-Free (844) 2REDEEM (273-3336)

Redemption Press is honored to present this title in partnership with the author. The views expressed or implied in this work are those of the author. Redemption Press provides our imprint seal representing design excellence, creative content, and high-quality production.

ISBN: 978-1-64645-224-8 (Paperback)
978-1-64645-225-5 (ePub)
978-1-64645-226-2 (Mobi)

Library of Congress Catalog Card Number: 2020916531

# Dedication

To my family:

Those who were with me from the beginning and those
who I met along the way.
Those related by blood and those related by love.
Thank you for lifting me up and carrying me through
this process.
This testimony is dedicated to you.

# contents

# author's note

I NEVER REALLY FELT ACCEPTED. I can't think of a single time in my life when I truly felt like I belonged. There was always a little part of me that felt like I wasn't supposed to be there or that I wasn't truly in the right place—whether it was my career, my family, or with friends. I struggled with feeling I was never good enough, like I never measured up. Even though I may have appeared to be successful, I never felt satisfied. No matter what I did or tried, I never felt good enough.

As I moved into my mid and late twenties, as with most of us, I started to truly understand who I am. I explored what characteristics defined who I am, how I viewed myself, the way the world viewed me, and the hurts and hang-ups that shaped me.

Perhaps you've done the same. Who we are and the way we think about ourselves become central to what we consider to be our identity. In turn, our identity is influenced by what we allow it to be influenced by. If that's our friends, then we care deeply about what our friends say about us. If it's our career, then we care deeply about that next promotion or the title or value of the impact of our work. In short, we seek value from others that we can only get from God.

In 2010 I began searching for my biological parents, thinking it might fill the void about who I was by finding them, or at least finding out more about them. There were obvious things like medical information or answering questions about my ethnicity that I'd never had answers to, but there were also questions of personality and preferences that I simply didn't know. Did I take after my mother or father? Did I inherit his laugh or her knack for organizing? I just didn't know, and it felt like a gap in who I was, a gap in my identity.

After years of searching on and off for them, the same years I spent changing jobs, exploring new hobbies, having a family of my own, and traveling, I came up with nothing. I felt just as unsatisfied as I did when I started my search. I wanted to give up. It felt as if I would never know where I came from and that I would always have a gap in knowing who I was. It's also important to note that during this time, I did not know Jesus. I believed in Him and I would go so far as to say I loved Him, but I did not have a relationship with Him.

Looking back now, nearly ten years later, I see that I was searching for my identity and my purpose from earthly things: other people, my job, my family, friends, money, success, stuff, my weight, my ability to make a family and create a home. Perhaps you too struggle with these things.

In 2014, while I was pregnant with our second child, my husband and I started attending a new church. It was during that year I came to know the Lord in a way I hadn't before. I can't remember a time I didn't believe in God, yet I hadn't been in a relationship with Him until late in that same year. During 2014 and the three years that followed, I grew closer and closer to Jesus. I learned how to fill that gaping hole in my life. Only God was able to quench my thirst, to truly understand who I was. To know God is to know *whose* you are. Know whose you are, and you can learn *who* you are . . . His.

Once I knew the Lord and knew who I was in Christ, things changed dramatically for me. I had given up on finding my birth parents. But then one day things really changed. All of a sudden, God placed people in my life, a stir in my heart, and a clear path to find my birth parents. A path never before seen, suddenly available and clearly illuminated by Him. I experienced a series of powerful, profound, and truly transformational events over the course of three short months. Only after I had placed my worth, my value, and my identity in the Lord did He lay out what I had started searching for—my earthly identity. It was only when I had placed my eternal identity first in God that He, in turn, fulfilled my desire to find my biological family. I had to put Him first. But He was not done with me. He had something even bigger in mind.

It's a surreal experience, the first time you realize God is asking you to do something for Him. I was driving home from the gym one evening, after another attempt at restorative yoga (hint: it's not for me). I remember being frustrated that I had just spent an hour trying to relax when so much was happening in my life, and being unable to let go just long enough to breathe. I started praying from that place of frustration when it clearly, and seemingly out of nowhere, occurred to me I was supposed to share my testimony. And not just share with anyone.

I was to write about it.

Broadly.

Publicly.

It clearly occurred to me in that moment I was to write a book.

This might not have been too weird or surprising for someone who, perhaps, was an established author. However, I was not. Not even close.

So I laughed. Out loud. It seemed so preposterous and so absurd—I didn't know what else to do but to laugh. The funny thing is, over the next several weeks, as I was sharing about the recent events with some close friends, every single person I shared with immediately said the exact same words to me: "You should write a book." God was affirming His directive to me through other people.

God has a funny way of getting my attention. He knows me. He knows I need a big flashing sign or a swing over the head with a two-by-four. I have a tough time with subtle hints—He knows it—and through these people, He showed me He was serious. I was called to write about my experience. This book you have in your hands is the result of nearly three years of slow, steady obedience to the Lord's calling. You may be here with me on these pages because you're adopted, or perhaps you're a birth or adoptive parent. Or perhaps you are simply looking to better understand your identity in the Lord. Whatever reason you have come to read these pages, I am so glad you are here. I don't believe it's an accident.

Throughout my story I will share more about what God says about us, about who we are, and about why we matter to Him. I will also share my personal journey about my family, my adoption, and ultimately my reunion with my birth parents and extended biological family. Remember—this came about only after I grew closer to God, turned to Him for my identity, my purpose, and my path to reunion. I hope through reading the pages in this book, you too will find peace with who you are, understanding about how God has created you and your family, and the ability to accept God's love for you, as His chosen son or daughter.

For years I did not believe God could love me. I didn't believe the Lord would love someone who wasn't created with intention, whose life on this earth was, by all human accounts, accidental. I lived believing that truth for thirty-three years. What I hope you come to learn through this book is that each and every one of us is chosen by God. No matter what the circumstances, He has predestined you according to His purpose for your life and loves you (Ephesians 1:3–14).

Each chapter will walk through a characteristic that God has outlined about us in Ephesians, a piece of my personal story, reflection questions for you to work through, action steps, and affirmations. These could be completed individually, with a friend or loved one, or in a small group. I encourage you to dig deep and search the depths of your soul to tap in to your true feelings and to accept the love of Jesus Christ. I pray the words on these pages help you feel the love of Jesus and help you find peace in the identity God has given you.

You, friend, are chosen.

# chapter one

## ADOPTED & ASHAMED

*And the man and his wife were both naked
and were not ashamed.*
Genesis 2:25

I HAD A BONE TO PICK with the Christian faith.

Now don't get me wrong—I believed in God and mostly believed in Jesus, although I didn't really understand it all.

I wasn't an atheist.

I loved God and believed in Him. He had carried me through several tough times in the past.

I wasn't against the principles or the message I heard in church.

I believed in most of what I heard in services—when I went.

But when that preacher lady (or man) stood in front

of the congregation and started talking about our purpose, our calling, it didn't resonate with me. You know what I mean—when they start getting all Romans 8:28—"And we know that God causes everything to work together for the good of those who love God and are called according to his purpose for them"—on you.

Well . . .

That's where I sorta stopped tracking.

I would always think, *Yeah maybe for you, but not me.*

*That's not my reality.*

*That's not my truth.*

My entire life, I had known one fact about how I came into this world, and it was not on purpose.

I was an accident.

There was no plan when it came to my conception. That I knew for sure.

Born as the product of teen pregnancy, I deeply struggled with this teaching about purpose. God created you on purpose, for a purpose?

Seriously? Tell that to the teen mom who gave me up at sixteen years old. Tell that to the birth father who wasn't involved. I don't think they would see purpose there either—other than broken hearts.

I wrestled with this concept for years. As far as I knew, my biological mother and father were dating at the time I was conceived but certainly did not purposefully plan to get pregnant. Shortly after I was conceived, they broke up. The details are a bit fuzzy for both parties as far as I know.

Let me back up.

I was born in December 1983 and adopted nine days after my birth by loving parents who raised me as their own flesh and blood. My father was also adopted and from day one wanted me to know I was adopted so there would be no surprises. My mother fully supported this approach, and therefore I cannot remember a single day of my life that I did not know I was adopted.

In my early years, being adopted didn't seem out of the ordinary at all. It seemed as normal as saying I had brown eyes or that I was right-handed. Being adopted was just one descriptor of who I was, and I did not feel like it made me different or unique in any way.

However, because I grew up looking different than my older-than-average parents, it wasn't uncommon for me to be asked one of two questions: "Are those your grandparents?" or bluntly, "Are you adopted?"

Not kidding. Kids are not exactly the most thoughtful or considerate. I am tall and have dark hair and dark-brown eyes, whereas my parents are both fair skinned: my father with red hair and green eyes, my mom blond and blue-eyed. They were thirty-eight and thirty-nine years old, respectively, when I was born, and as such, I was raised an only child by older parents. After one or both of those first couple of questions would come, I'd wait, because next was almost always some form of the same question: "So do you want to meet your birth parents?"

Sigh.

Sometimes it was as insensitive as "So do you want to meet your *real* parents?"

Real parents?

As if my adoptive parents were just stand-ins or some kind of fake parents.

It still stings writing these words. I'd remind the askers

that these "*are* my 'real' parents." The ones who kissed boo-boos and looked under the bed for monsters. The ones who grounded me for being late for curfew and who said yes to the man who asked for my hand in marriage.

These are my real parents.

The ones who raised me.

My mom and my dad.

Tee and Bill.

For years this was the end of the story. I had two loving parents. I didn't need to, or want to, find my biological parents. Especially if they'd made a choice to remove themselves from my life. Who was I to undo that? And for what purpose? I didn't have a reason to open that door, so I didn't.

## Adoption and Shame

Adoption is a tough topic for a million reasons. The emotions, the circumstances—they are complicated and different for everyone. I think the unsaid truth about adoption for most is that it wasn't the first choice. It's hard for me to type these words and put them on this page, because I know they hurt. They hurt me, and they may also hurt you. They aren't warm and fuzzy, and they certainly don't make anyone particularly comfortable to say out loud. But for many of us, they are true.

Usually (but admittedly, not always) there are a few things that happen with adoption. There is a person or a couple who want to have a baby and can't, and there is a person who is having, or had, a baby who either cannot or does not want to keep the baby, and then there is the baby itself. This group of people, often referred to as the adoption triad, is the union between the birth parents, adoptee, and adoptive parents. The triad is wound tight with so many complex emotions. For me, underneath several softer emotions, I mostly felt shame.

Shame is a big, heavy emotion defined as "a painful feeling of humiliation or distress caused by consciousness of wrong or foolish behavior."[1] As the adoptee in my particular situation, I was aware that my existence was the result of what society would likely describe as wrong or foolish behavior. Certainly, the church, the Bible, and most people I knew would agree with that. Adoptees feel shame for two big reasons: they were perceived to be unwanted by their birth parents (regardless of truth) and they were the second choice to their adoptive parents (also regardless of truth).

Additionally, the remaining members of the adoption triad face their own brand of shame. Society puts a lot of pressure on the family unit. Almost from the moment a couple is married, the questions start rolling in regarding when children will join the picture. Unfortunately, when things do not go the "normal" way, many of us feel shame. Adoptive parents feel shame for not being able to get pregnant like "everybody else." Birth parents feel shame for getting pregnant when they did not desire to, often facing judgment of their parents, peers, and even complete strangers. Those are not popular statements, I realize. And I recognize they may not be true for every situation. Yet many of us believe these things to be true about ourselves or others.

---

[1] https://www.lexico.com/en/definition/shame, accessed February 6, 2020.

## Shame in the Garden

We can trace shame all the way back to the beginning of humanity. In Genesis we see God created a beautiful garden where everything was good and there was no sin. The world existed peacefully, and humanity was at peace with one another and with God. But then mankind decided to try life apart from God, by disobeying His guidance and making their own decisions by eating the fruit from the tree that God told them not to.

We've all done this. We have all done something we know we're not supposed to, which pulls us apart from God's guidance and leads us to sin. In the garden, Adam and Eve made the decision to believe that who they were with God wasn't enough—they desired more than God. They took things into their own hands, sinned, and felt shame.

Before sin, the Bible clearly states in Genesis 2:25 that "the man and his wife were naked and were not ashamed." After sin, Adam and Eve hid from God in the garden because they became very aware of their sin and were ashamed.

In the same way Adam and Eve felt shame, I too felt ashamed. As a small child, I always knew I was adopted, but it was the only truth I knew, and I didn't realize it was different. Much like Adam and Eve were naked and not ashamed, as a child I was adopted and not ashamed. It felt normal to me. However, as I grew up, I learned that not everyone was adopted, and further, that it wasn't as common as I'd thought. At a young age, I knew many adopted people because my parents were friends with many other people who also adopted kids. As I became a teenager, I learned that not only was adoption not the norm but was something to be made fun of. Yes, I was teased for being adopted. Perhaps you were too.

## Unwanted

The summer before my freshman year of high school, at the impressionable age of fourteen, I was enjoying a quiet evening of dial-up internet via AOL. A boy from my class sent me an IM (instant message). At first, it seemed harmless enough, so I willingly engaged in what seemed like an innocent conversation. He was with a friend, and they began saying unkind things to me about how I didn't belong. They told me I didn't look like my parents and started questioning me on why that was. They asked me if my parents were my grandparents. I explained that no, they weren't my grandparents but that I was adopted, which was why I didn't look like them. *No big deal*, I thought.

Wrong.

I guess it was a big deal.

To this day I will never forget the exact words they used, but for the sake of staying on the G-rated side of things, let's just paraphrase: no one must like me, especially my parents, since they "got rid of me." The exact ending was: "No one wants you or likes you. Not even your parents."

I sat on the other side of the computer screen and cried. I cried for long, long time that night, and I cried many times over the years that followed. I let what those bullies said sink into my heart and carve a home in my brain. I did not have a defensible position, I thought. I was adopted. My birth parents did give me away. I didn't know why they gave me up. I just knew they did. Perhaps this was true.

Unwanted.

Second choice.

Simply filling a void for two people unable to fill in their preferred way.

Deep shame set in. I was now adopted and very ashamed.

Worst of all, I suspected perhaps this was true for God too. If He was real, how could He love me, when I wasn't supposed to be here? When I am a second choice? When I am an accident? Maybe I wasn't His choice or a part of His plan either.

Maybe I wasn't anyone's choice.

Maybe I wasn't anyone's plan.

The truth is, I wasn't unwanted, not in the least. But that didn't stop me from believing the words spoken to me by my peers. The Enemy has an interesting way of making us feel ashamed instead of feeling ashamed of the sin. In this case, I felt ashamed to be adopted instead of feeling ashamed of the sin that led to my conception and eventual adoption. This shame felt a lot like rejection both by my birth parents and by my peers, who thought it was super fun to point out how unloved I was and that my birth parents gave me away. As Lysa TerKeurst says in her book *Uninvited*, "The enemy loves to take our rejection and twist it into raw, irrational fear that God really doesn't have a good plan for us."[2] Truth bomb. That was exactly how I felt.

## God's Plan > Our Plan

We need to remember that even though adoption may not have been our plan, it was part of God's plan. As an

---

[2] Lysa TerKeurst, *Uninvited* (Nashville: Thomas Nelson, 2016), 129.

adoptee I found it hard to accept that my adoptive parents first attempted to have biological children of their own, and when that did not work out, they then chose adoption. Feeling like (or *being*) their second choice for how they created a family is a complex thing to wrestle with. The key word here is *their*. It was their second choice for how *they* wanted to have children. We have to remember—God's plan is perfect. He planned our lives long before we were born. This is always God's plan for us—we are planned for.

The same is true for how I feel about my birth parents. True, they did not plan to have me. At sixteen and seventeen years old, they were not intending to get pregnant. But God knew it would happen, and God made plans for me. God made plans for you too. God does not make mistakes. As Paul wrote in Romans 8:28–29 (NLT), "And we know that God causes everything to work together for the good of those who love God and are called according to his purpose for them. For God knew his people in advance, and he chose them to become like his Son, so that his Son would be the firstborn among many brothers and sisters." There is so much goodness and freedom for us in these two verses.

First, the emphasis is on who makes everything work together. Very clearly Paul states, "God causes everything to work together." The important thing to note here is that it is reserved for those who love God. Romans 8:28 is explicit that for those who love Him, the outcome is positive. You might be thinking, *Okay, but it doesn't feel beneficial. I am still hurting.* Rest in knowing that the verse does not say when; it just says it works together. Take heart—your story isn't over, this isn't the end, and God will cause your story to work together too. I had no idea what God was up to, but I was about to find out.

## Carrying the Cross

In April of 2010, I was twenty-six years old, married, newly pregnant, and had stuffed the shame of my adoption deep down inside my heart. It was so deep, I didn't even recognize it as shame anymore. I believed the comments made by the bullies. I believed the comments made about me by family members that I wasn't a "true heir" because I was adopted—that I wasn't really family. I read stories about adoption that made it seem like rainbows and butterflies, without mention of the complexities of the emotions on all sides. It was as if after the baby was united with the adoptive parents, the adoption received a perfect little checkmark and everyone was to go off and live happily ever after. That's simply not true.

For nearly three decades I made these feelings and the harsh words said about adoption, about me, my personal truths. My personal cross. I let these things people said to me or about me become my reality and my identity. I chose to believe them.

That is precisely the problem. I believed everyone and everything else above God. I looked to the wrong place to find my identity, my value, and my worth. It was from this place that I was struggling. Struggling to know just who I was. Struggling to strive for acceptance, approval, and true love. It did not feel like everything was working together. Quite the opposite, in fact. I was up for a promotion at work, had just started a graduate degree program, was questioning myself and who I was, all the while pregnant and about to become a mom for the first time.

I was only six weeks pregnant but already found myself thinking about my birth mother and what it was like for her, knowing she was carrying a baby and was going to give her away—give me away. I couldn't imagine what that must have felt like. I already felt so connected to my baby. For the first time, I found myself wondering about her. I could feel that there was some amount of small change—something stirring deep, deep down in my heart. This little seed of curiosity sprouted roots, and my interest grew. Things were about to change.

## Reflection

### Questions

1. How would you describe who you are?
2. Who have you let define who you are? If not God, why not?
3. When have you felt apart or separated from God? What was life like then?

### Affirmations

1. God loves me and created me exactly how I am.
2. God has a plan for me.
3. I am enough just how God made me.

# *chapter two*

## THE LETTER

*God created everything through him,
and nothing was created except through him.*
John 1:3 NLT

M Y MOM HAD ASKED ME TO come to her house. By
this time, we had lost my father to a long fight with
cancer, and she was living alone. We lived about a mile
apart off the same major road, and stopping over to visit
her was relatively easy. When it was nice out, I could walk
there. That particular day I drove the short distance and
wondered what it was that she wanted to visit about. She
had been vague on the phone, and I never knew what that
could mean.

It was a beautiful warm spring day, the kind that makes
you feel sure winter is finally over and summer is just
around the corner. Growing up in Iowa, spring can be just

a blip on the radar between long, snowy winters and blistering-hot summer. This particular day had a slight breeze and a warm, soothing undertone that smelled of freshly cut grass. I drove with my window down and let the breeze blow through my long hair. Spring was here, and it felt oh so good. I realized I was smiling—ear to ear. It was going to be hard to keep the secret from her.

We were six weeks pregnant.

I pulled into my mom's driveway and shut the door to my SUV. The street was empty and quiet except for a few robins chirping in the neighbor's lawn. I let out a breath and walked toward her door. She was waiting for me, holding open the storm door. I walked into the house, and she gave me a hug as we exchanged hellos and made our way to the sunroom, which had beautiful French doors propped open and large windows on the three remaining walls. As she eased down onto her chair, I nervously sat across from her on the sofa, my right foot tucked under my left leg to keep it from twitching. Her lips pressed together, and she glanced at me. I looked at her blankly, not wanting her to know I was keeping something from her. She was good at knowing when something was up. Without saying a word, she reached for the table and picked up a large letter-sized envelope I hadn't noticed among the *National Geographic* magazines stacked in their usual place on the coffee table.

"There's something I want to go through with you," she said, finally breaking the silence. She looked me in the eye and seemed a bit uncomfortable. I realized her cheeks were a bit splotchy—in the way her fair skin showed when she was nervous. She held the yellowed envelope in one hand and pushed her glasses up her nose with the other.

"What is it?" I asked.

"Well, it's your papers. From your adoption. You've seen them before, but I want to go through it with you and then let you take it home with you for good. It's mostly stuff from the lawyer and a few other things."

I noticed a small plastic grocery bag sitting next to the magazines.

My lips were separated, and I realized my jaw had dropped a little bit. I did not see that coming—not at all. I realized I too was flushed. Mom was right—she had shared the information with me before, just not in its entirety, not the full file. She reached over and handed me the yellowed letter-sized envelope. As I reached for it, I could smell the musk of the papers, like an old, damp basement. My hands grasped on to the worn edges, and I looked over the type-writer lettering on the front envelope. It was our home address from back in 1983, the year I was born.

In my mom's handwriting, "investigation" was written sideways on the upper left-hand corner in faded, but still blue, pen. The file was thicker than I'd expected. I ran my fingers across the yellowed envelope, unsure what to expect to find inside. I wrapped my fingers around the side of the envelope and under the unsealed flap. As I went to open the envelope, my mother shifted her weight forward in the chair and reached up to her face to push her glasses up her nose again—fingers on one side and thumb on the other. She fidgeted this way when she was nervous or uncomfortable.

She opened her mouth as I flipped the envelope flap open. She paused but then spoke.

"There's a letter," she said flatly. She looked at me, holding her tongue, waiting for me to react. She shifted her weight back in the chair now, then rubbed the palms of her hands up and down her thighs, on top of her jeans.

I looked down at the envelope and stopped. "What do you mean, a letter?"

Silence reigned for a moment. Mom stopped moving her hands and exhaled. She hesitated. "Well," she started slowly, "when you were adopted, I was told that your birth mom's mother wrote you a letter that you could get when you turned eighteen. The attorney has it—I forget her name—K something. Her name is in the files. You should try to get it."

There was a long pause while I repeated what she had just said in my head over and over again.

A letter. From my biological maternal grandmother. For me.

I could feel my heart pounding in my chest and my face flushing a deep shade of red.

*I don't understand.*

There was a letter from my grandmother. I felt like there were questions I wanted to ask, but they were all stuck in my throat. A letter from my grandmother. A woman I had never thought about. I couldn't get any of my thoughts to make sense . . . no questions would come together. I felt paralyzed. I sat there, grasping the envelope, unable to move.

After some amount of time, I put thoughts together. I couldn't tell you if it was five seconds or five minutes that passed. I could feel my heart pounding in my ears as I rubbed my forehead and began to process what Mom had just shared with me.

"Um," I started. "Okay. I'm not really sure what to say. I will read the papers, and then can I ask questions later?"

"Yes, of course. Of course. Anytime." Mom stood and handed me the plastic grocery bag. "These were from her too—these toys. I think they were from the gift shop at the hospital. Christmas themed, since it was near the holidays."

"Thanks. I'll take them—I'll take them home." I took the bag in my right hand and grasped the envelope with my left arm. I felt as if the world was moving in slow motion, like I was walking through a cloud.

I was stunned.

*Why am I just learning about this now?* I thought. *I'm twenty-six, not eighteen.*

I couldn't bring myself to ask. I was too shocked to ask questions.

My mom and I finished talking and hugged goodbye. I knew we did, but everything just felt so surreal, like I was having an out-of-body experience. I walked out of her house, down the front steps, and out to my car in a daze. My thoughts were foggy. I wasn't sure how much was pregnancy fog or the shock of what I'd just learned. I fumbled with the keyless entry, opened the door, and sat down in the driver's seat. I inserted my key into the ignition and turned on the car to cool it down from the hot sun. For a few moments, I sat blankly staring out the windshield, parked in my mom's driveway. I leaned back in the hot leather seat. I had left the sunroof open, and the sun's heat had made the leather warm enough to stick to my skin.

There was something in that letter—there had to be. Something important. Something that my grandmother wanted me to know. You didn't just write a letter for the sake of writing the letter, right? One that would be given, or was intended to be given, to the person eighteen years later? There was a purpose to that letter. Something she wanted me to know or do or have. What could she have said? There was something out there, a message, from my grandmother that she wanted me to know. I suddenly felt the need to try to find her, to find out what it was.

And that feeling was brand new.

That seed of curiosity in my heart was watered, and it was starting to grow.

I needed to find that letter.

## My Earthly Adoption

Until then, I'd never thought about searching for my biological family—not even a little bit. I had been asked enough times over the years to know how I felt about it, or so I thought. I did ponder about them occasionally, but never about trying to track them down.

Since I only knew my dad "wasn't involved," I assumed he was a jerk who got his girlfriend pregnant and bailed— and who does that? Abandons their girlfriend and unborn child? Because of this, I had zero interest in finding him. Now, do I believe people can change? Of course I do. But I also knew plenty of jerks (read: college). That was about the extent of my feelings about my biological dad for many years. At that moment, those feelings remained the same. I didn't need or want to find him.

However, even as a kid, I visualized what my birth mom would look like. Since she was only a little under seventeen years older than me, I had this fantasy-like vision we

would look similar—more like sisters than mother-daugh-
ter. In that fantasy, we shared the same taste, had similar
interests, and looked a lot alike—no—almost the identi-
cal, only with her being slightly more aged. She too would
have long, nearly black hair, brown eyes, and olive skin. Of
course, we would be the same height and weight—almost
like looking in a mirror. I thought about her periodically,
what she might be doing, if she graduated college, had a career or a family of her own, and if they might know about
me. I found myself thinking about her on my birthday and
around hers most years. I knew her birthday from the paperwork my mom had showed me years ago.

I always had respect for her. To be sixteen, pregnant
(and probably not wanting to be), and to go through pregnancy, childbirth, and then give that baby—your baby—
away to someone else was just something I couldn't fathom
doing. I couldn't—still can't—imagine going through all of
that at sixteen, only to pick up life from there and carry on.
I hadn't yet given birth to this little baby growing inside of
me, and I already felt such a connection to it. Respect for
my birth mom, and what she had done, only grew since
becoming pregnant myself.

I had been told at some point that the maternal grandmother had been a nurse and wanted to keep me. She would
have been only a couple of years older than my adoptive
mother was. It wouldn't have been a huge stretch for her to
raise me as her own. So when I learned about the letter, this
only reinforced the story as I knew it: that she wanted me.

My adoptive parents, my mom and dad, had always
been open and transparent about my adoption. They'd al-

ways told me I was adopted. My dad had also been adopted. Back then, in the forties, adoption was never discussed openly because it was viewed by society as something to be ashamed of. Often, children were matched based on appearance, as my dad had been. Because of this practice, it was no surprise that my dad looked like a spitting image of his adoptive dad—down to their matching red hair and all-over freckles.

## Now What Do I Do?

That day as I drove slightly over a mile from my mom's house to our house, I was thankful—thankful for the short drive, thankful for the quiet, and oh so grateful for the time to begin to process the bomb that was just dropped on me. My mind went still as I drove silently west toward our town house. My sunglasses slid slightly down on the bridge of my nose, and I pushed them up with the back of my hand. I glanced over at the large yellowed envelope taking residence in the passenger seat.

Just as the little seed of a baby was growing in my belly, a seed of interest was growing in my heart. For the first time, I felt something beyond general curiosity about my biological parents.

I started to wonder what my dad would think about Mom telling me about this letter. I was twenty-six now, and he'd passed away seven years before after a long battle with esophageal cancer. Did he know about the letter? Did he want me to know about it? To have it? I would like to think he would—if it was what I wanted. He had always supported me, gave me every opportunity possible growing up. I could only assume he would support me in whatever would make me happy, whether that would be to pursue this letter or not. I wouldn't want to hurt either of my parents by searching for this letter, but why mention the letter and encourage me to find it if you didn't expect me to do something with it—to search?

I realized I had been sitting in my car idle in the driveway for a while, thinking about all those people who played a role creating my life and this mysterious letter. Twenty-six years this letter had existed and was known by everyone except for me.

It was a lot to swallow.

*David is never going to believe this*, I thought as I pulled the rest of the way into the garage and parked my car. I unlocked the car and opened the door. I walked up the four steps from the garage to the house and turned the doorknob. As I opened the door to our home, I noticed David was at the sink finishing up the dishes from the night before. He turned around and smiled.

"So?" he asked, turning off the water and reaching for the dishtowel draped over his shoulder, water droplets falling off his hands. "What did she want?"

"You are never going to believe this. There's a letter," I began. "A letter from my maternal grandmother that I was supposed to get at eighteen."

I paused.

"Babe, it gets better. Mom gave me this." I held up the yellowed letter-sized envelope containing all my adoption records. "This is all of my adoption paperwork."

He paused mid-toweling of his hands. Just as shocked

as I had been an hour before, he tossed the towel on the countertop in a heap, not bothering to fold it. His eyebrows lifted, and he paused briefly.

"Wow." He drew in a long breath and crossed his arms. "She has to know we're pregnant. Why else would she bring this up now, after all these years? You said you were supposed to get this letter at eighteen, so has she known about this letter the whole time?"

"I don't know. I guess she must have. I don't know why she waited to tell me—I am in shock, I think—I didn't ask a lot of questions. I just didn't know where to start."

There was a long quiet. We were both processing.

His eyes gazed from mine to the envelope I was holding tightly against my chest.

"What's in the file?" He uncrossed his arms and pointed at the envelope.

"Oh, all kinds of stuff. Sit down," I said, gesturing to our kitchen table. We sat down, and I described what was in the envelope and what the conversation with my mom had been like. As we poured through all the papers and forms, we read everything from recommendations about my parents from friends, to bills they paid for my birth mother's hospital stay, to attorney's fees, to the official final court order from July 3, 1984, making my adoption final. There were also notes—so many notes—from my mom on everything from phone calls to little facts she had pried out of the attorney about what happened throughout the process and about my birth parents.

As we finished going through the paperwork, David stacked everything neatly together in a pile and tucked them back inside the envelope—like a twenty-six-year-old time capsule. He leaned back in his chair, and his eyes locked with mine.

"So. The million-dollar question: What are you going to do?" he asked. "I'll support you in whatever you decide."

After a long pause, I shifted my weight in the chair across the table from his. "I don't know." I folded my arms against my chest. "But I am curious about what might be in that letter." I paused again. "I need to think about it. I had never considered searching for anything until now."

And I did. I pondered. I processed. I imagined.

For days.

Then weeks.

I thought about what it might say and what it might not say. I had so many questions. Were they even allowed to write a letter, given the adoption was private? Do attorneys keep things that long? Was it even real or just a rumor? How does one keep track of something for twenty-six years? I could barely remember what was on my to-do list, and how would an attorney remember a single letter from one of probably hundreds or thousands of cases decades prior? Even if it did exist, when I didn't get it at eighteen, did she get rid of it? Did I even want to know what it said? Could it be good—or possibly bad? I was sure the letter could not tell anything that would identify her—I was fairly certain that was prohibited merely based on the closed nature of the adoption.

I wrestled with the pursuit of the letter for months. I didn't know what I wanted to do or if I wanted to open the door. The key was—I wrestled. I did not pray. I did not consult. I took all those emotions, the processing and the emotional exploration that evoked from learning of the letter, and I let it fester inside me.

## Reflection

### Questions

1. What does it feel like to know you are adopted into God's family?
2. Knowing you belong to God's family, how can you share that acceptance with others?
3. Because this adoption cannot be earned, and it is for *everyone*, does that change how you feel toward others?
4. Does your perception of earthy adoption and biblical adoption align? Why or why not?

### Affirmations

1. No matter what my family is like on earth, I am part of God's family.
2. I am God's beloved child.
3. God has adopted me into His family, and I am a coheir with Jesus.

# chapter three

❦

## SEEKING

*In love, he predestined us for adoption to himself*
*as sons through Jesus Christ, according to the*
*purpose of his will.*
Ephesians 1:5 NLT

B Y NOW A FEW MONTHS HAD past, and I was about
halfway through my pregnancy. So much had happened to keep me distracted from moving forward with
searching for the letter. Crib shopping, figuring out car
seats, and taking birth classes, as well as managing through
a big promotion at work alongside my first year of grad
school. It was a lot, and things had just settled down long
enough for me to decide what I wanted to do.

I finally made up my mind.

I was going to search.

I was giddy and nervous and unsure what to expect,
but I knew I wanted to move forward. I knew I wanted

to find out who I was and where I came from. I knew I wanted to find them, my biological family.

For a while I sat hunched over the kitchen table simply looking down at the envelope. It's funny how something you've read before can suddenly come alive with all new intention and impact, like a quick snap of your fingers. I was still shocked by the news of the letter.

*Surprise!*

There's a letter from your birth family. A letter that contains something they wanted you to know. A letter my mother knew about for twenty-six years and never mentioned it to me once. I still couldn't believe it.

I lifted both hands out of my lap and picked up the envelope containing my adoption records, tipping it toward me. It smelled musty from years locked away. I sat the envelope down on the table, facing up, and unfolded the old cool metal clasp. I opened the top and pulled out the stack of papers within. It was a thick stack, maybe an inch or so high, mostly notes that either my mother had written or more formal documents from the attorney. I slowly flipped through each page, looking for clues as to where to start.

While I remembered seeing the envelope as a child, for the first time I noticed the file had all sorts of information tucked away, documents I didn't recall. There were financial records, letters attesting to my parents' character from friends who knew them well, reports from the social worker, notes from various appointments with the attorney, and my final adoption record from the court. My adoption was done privately, so no agency paperwork was included. I was a bit disappointed when I realized that was the case, as I knew that agencies sometimes helped adoptees with their searches.

I sat at the kitchen table for hours, flipping through the paperwork, trying to organize it into some sort of sequence or order for it to make sense. The documents were in a somewhat random order, and there were only two that seemed useful. The first was a one-page document with three columns: one for characteristics, one for birth mother, and one for birth father. It contained things like hair and eye color, height and weight, date of birth, what state they were born in, nationality, and known medical history. The medical history was somewhat light, given my birth parents were teenagers at the time of my birth; my birth mother sixteen, almost seventeen, and my birth father eighteen. The paper had more information about my birth mother than birth father, which matched my understanding that my birth father hadn't been involved. The other document contained names of the attorney, the doctor, and my parents—the official court record certifying my adoption. Between these two key papers, I thought I might make some progress.

When my mom gave me this envelope, she mentioned the attorney was supposed to have this letter and suggested I start with her. This woman worked with my parents and my birth mother and her parents twenty-six years ago. Twenty-six years! That sat heavily on my heart as I ran my index finger across her typed name. Karla Fultz. This was the woman who had the mysterious letter. She was the key—my starting point.

I let out a sigh and looked up at the table and the mess

of papers I had scattered about. This all felt heavy and surreal. There was a big part of me that couldn't get past that
just a few months ago, I had no interest in searching for my
birth parents. Yet here at my kitchen table, surrounded by
old yellowed documents, I had all this fresh information
and new interest in finding two people I knew existed my
entire life, yet had no interest in finding until now. I paused
for what felt like a long time, stood up court filing in hand,
and walked upstairs to my computer.

I decided I would start by searching the attorney's name
on Google.

A hit. Right away.

My heart raced, but my body stayed still.

*That was easy.* I inhaled slowly.

As I scrolled slowly, I clicked through several links and
read each carefully. She appeared to still be living and now
a juvenile court judge in the fifth district.

"Wow," I said out loud. "Here we go."

I jotted down her phone number and email address as
I heard my husband walk in the door from work. I couldn't
wait to tell him what I had found.

This just might be it.

## Coming Up Empty

The next day I called the office and left a message with
the administrative assistant about my search and what I
was looking for. She was kind and polite but let me know
it was unlikely that I would hear back anytime soon, as the
judge had a busy docket.

Months went by.

No response.

I followed up a few times both by phone and by email, but to no avail. I tried to find a way to contact her personally. As one might expect, finding personal information of a juvenile court judge isn't easy. I tried anything and everything I could think of. Finally I tracked her down on Facebook. By now it had been ten months since my mom had shared my file with me and we had welcomed our first child into the world. I sent the judge a Facebook message on March 31, 2011, but didn't hear back. Things got a bit busy as a new family of three. I changed jobs, and as time went by, my search seemed less and less likely to pan out. I didn't know what else to do, given finding the letter was what I was most interested in.

Then on June 13, 2011, two and a half months later and over a year since I learned about the letter, I received a response: "I will check and see if I have any old files. Generally, they are only maintained 10 years. I'm sorry not to have responded sooner, but I don't check Facebook often."

I wanted to be excited, overjoyed perhaps, or at least encouraged. While I felt a little disappointed, I mostly felt . . . nothing. I leaned back in my chair, surprised by my own emotions. Looking back now, I think I was trying to protect myself from yet more disappointment and heartbreak.

What was I searching for?

After twenty-six years of not desiring to find my birth parents, learning about one letter completely upended my desire. I was questioning myself. Questioning my own motives. I sat in this feeling for weeks. Unsure of myself. Unsure of my reasons for searching. Unsure of what I might find or why I wanted to find out who they were.

I second-guessed everything. I was afraid to find they weren't alive. Afraid to find out they didn't want anything to do with me. Afraid to find out my birth was actually worse than just two teenagers making a mistake. Could I be the result of abuse? Would my birth parents be normal everyday people? Or addicts or in jail? Sick or well? Was opening this door really the right thing?

I responded to the judge within an hour of hearing from her, but never heard from her again. I took this as my sign that it wasn't meant to be.

And I let it go.

## Searching for Wholeness

Over the three years that followed this initial disappointment, from 2011 to 2014, my husband changed jobs and I left public accounting to pursue auditing in the corporate world. I graduated from my first master's degree program, we moved twice, and the list goes on. Every year and a half to two years, I would get this stirring I couldn't explain. I would feel unsettled, either with my career or our home or some other aspect of our life, and I would seek satisfaction, wholeness, completion in . . . something. I was fortunate to get promoted several times during this five-year period. I changed companies—twice—and began my second master's degree.

It looked pretty good from the outside.

It was good. Our lives would check all the boxes in the so-called American dream.

But I wasn't good.

I was searching for fulfillment.

No matter how many roles I had as a wife, mother, daughter, mentor, mentee, leader, or employee, I never felt complete. I never felt whole. Nothing I did or achieved filled the hole in my identity that I tried to stuff with anything seemingly good. No amount of achievement or accomplishment, no praise or success, filled the gap. The harsh truth was, I didn't know who I was or how to feel whole on my own. I wore different hats, but deep down I was lost, and I hid it well. Behind the veil of accomplishments, perfectly clean house, successful career, and smiling photos was a woman who wasn't sure what made her who she was or how to fill the gaping hollow in her heart.

## Still Searching

Around this same time, my husband and I set out to try and find a new church home. We had been attending church somewhat regularly since we had been married but both felt like it wasn't a great fit for us. We kept hearing about a particular church from many people urging us to try it. On Palm Sunday 2014, while we were pregnant with our second child, we finally did. Admittedly, we were reluctant to try it given it was huge. Turned out it happened to be the largest Lutheran church in America. As we entered the front doors, people greeted us warmly and welcomed us. We navigated the crowd and took a seat for our first sermon at Lutheran Church of Hope. Ironically, hope was just what I was looking for.

We settled in and absorbed the size of the crowd and

said hello to the people seated next to us. As the band ended the opening song, a pastor took the stage. In his opening announcements, he said the weirdest thing. "We believe it's no accident that you're here, and we've been praying for you."

My smile faded and my jaw dropped. I could feel the color slowly drain out of my face. The statement hit me like the proverbial ton of bricks.

*I'm pretty sure it's an accident I'm here. I shouldn't even be alive.*

Yeah . . . dark, right?

I had no idea what was said after that first statement. My whole life I'd believed I was an accident. I think any of us could come to that conclusion rather easily if we were looking at the circumstances. Two teenagers get pregnant. Not intentionally. Thus, an accident. Since the pregnancy resulted in my birth, I am an accident.

This did not feel too farfetched. In fact, I had always believed this to be true. It was a central theme in who I believed I was. Born by accident and given away at birth. Adopted by parents who wanted *any* baby. Not me specifically, but any baby. If you're adopted, perhaps you have felt this emptiness too.

Because of this core opinion, I struggled to believe my life was created on purpose, for a purpose. Every day of my life, I believed this to be my truth. As Paul wrote in Romans 8:28, "And we know that for those who love God, all things work together for good, for those who are called according to his purpose." I wanted to believe this was true—that there was purpose for my life, purpose for me. It sounded nice. But I felt so unworthy, unplanned for, accidental, that I could not wrap my heart or my mind around the idea that God had a plan or a purpose for my life. I believed this was true for others but not for me.

## Orphaned

When we are aligned with God's truth, we live a life loved. We live as His beloved sons and daughters. When we are *misaligned*, we are walking on our own path, either not with God or willingly ignoring His guidance, and we don't experience the full love of Jesus Christ. In short, when we walk without God, we live an orphaned life. *By choice.*

> God decided in advance to adopt us into his own family by bringing us to himself through Jesus Christ. This is what he wanted to do and it gave him great pleasure. (Ephesians 1:5)

As an adoptee, you don't have a choice about your adoption. You simply *are* adopted, whether you want to be or not. It is something that happens to you and is a part of you in an earthly sense. But in Christ, we all have a choice. It is not something that just happens to us. We can choose to live life as an orphan or a life adopted. It all comes down to this: Do you want a life adopted into the family of the Most High? As God's heir, equal to Jesus Christ? A life with God, the only perfect Father, as your heavenly Father? Or do you want to continue a life as an orphan, apart from God?

It is a choice.

It is my choice.

It is your choice.

But it is a choice.

When I had this aha moment, it was the word *orphaned* that really struck me. Whether I wanted to admit it or not, that word had always stung. I'm not sure if it's because I lost my father at nineteen to cancer and was afraid I would lose my mother too, leaving me an orphan, or if I was hypersensitive to it because of my birth parents giving me up for adoption. Perhaps it was both. Either way, when I first realized walking without God was choosing to be an orphan, I knew I did not want that. I wanted to be a part of God's love, a part of His plan, and a part of His family. I wanted God's adoption. I wanted to feel the truth promised in Ephesians. I wanted to feel wanted. I wanted to feel loved—not as a second choice or a second option, but as *the* choice.

As Paul explains, God does just that. He "decided in advance to adopt us." Note it does not say "decided in advance after His other plan didn't quite work out." It does not say "decided in advance because something happened to Him." He decided in advance to choose us because it was His plan to adopt us all along. God chose *adoption first* for us. As Paul wrote in Romans:

> For all those led by God's Spirit are God's sons. For you did not receive a spirit of slavery to fall back into fear. Instead, you received the Spirit of adoption, by whom we cry out Abba, Father! The Spirit himself testifies together with our spirit that we are God's children, and if

children, also heirs of God and coheirs with
Christ—if indeed we suffer with him so that
we may also be glorified with him." (Romans
8:14–17 CSB)

In this explanation of adoption, we are given equal status with Jesus. There is no exception, no footnote, no qualifier. This means we can place our identity and our status in
God instead of letting other people, society, and the world
define who we are. We need to deeply challenge ourselves
and the source of that value. Are you valuing what others
believe, when the only thing that matters is what God be-
lieves about you? As Paul wrote in Galatians 1:10 (CSB), "If
I were still trying to please people, I would not be a servant of Christ." Therefore, if you are trying to please people
through works or who you are, you are trying to obtain
acceptance from the world and will never be satisfied.

## Why We Matter

It is so easy to get caught up in the swirl of life, only to
be met with the humble realization of how small our part
really is. With billions of people in the world, how can we
individually matter? How can we matter to God?

When we compare our little slice of life to those around
us, it's easy to fall into the thought patterns of *they have it
better* or *they do more* or *they are more significant than I am.*
It can become a habit, and that toxic thought process can
bring us down. The Enemy loves this. It gives power to our
doubts and power of darkness over the light. We begin to
doubt ourselves, our worth, and ultimately our significance
in this world.

We were not put on this planet to compare ourselves to each other. We were put on this earth to serve the Lord. When we get these two confused, doubt, fear, and self-importance creep in, threatening to overthrow our purpose.

When you fully grasp your value and worth in Him, then what other people say about you no longer matters.

God promises us more. He created us in His image (Psalm 8:5; Genesis 1:27) and gave us each a purpose (Romans 8:28). If God's Word is true, then we are hardly insignificant to Him. He created us in His image because we matter to Him.

## Reflection

### Questions

1. What does true and unconditional acceptance look like?
2. How can you show unconditional love and acceptance toward others?
3. Is it hard for you to accept that God has chosen you? Why or why not?

### Affirmations

1. No matter what I have done or will do, God loves me.
2. There is nothing I can do to prevent God from seeking me.
3. God is with me always.

# PARENTED BY GOD

*This means that anyone who belongs to Christ*
*has become a new person. The old life is gone;*
*a new life has begun.*
2 Corinthians 5:17 NLT

THE NEXT WEEKEND WAS EASTER, AND as we sat in church service, the announcements featured an upcoming class called Alpha. I had heard of this before from others who had taken the class. With the deep desire to grow in my faith before our second child was born (due just five months later), I mentioned to David I wanted to attend. Since the Alpha course is offered all over the world and is a simple week-by-week breakdown of Christianity, that seemed to be exactly what I was looking for. He encouraged me to sign up. He also expressed interest, but given the timing of our pregnancy and the course length, he offered to take it after me so we could balance taking the class and managing the kids. I pulled out my phone and signed up for the course through the church website.

The course started the following week on Wednesday and worked perfectly because I could go from work directly to church. Each week the course started with a meal, where we sat with our breakout groups and got to know each other better. The first night, I was delighted to meet other women my age in my breakout group who were also searching for more. As the course progressed, I learned about Jesus, God, the Bible, and how to have faith. For the first time in my life, I felt like Christianity wasn't just for other people. I felt like I could ask questions, as basic as they may be, and feel at ease and welcomed instead of intimidated and lost. The people in the Alpha ministry taught me God would meet me where I was and would walk with me as my faith grew.

For the first time, I purchased a Bible and began reading it. I started praying regularly and reaffirmed my baptism the last night of the class. I wanted to better understand God's love, why He did what He did by sending Jesus to earth, and how to apply His Word to my life. It was during Alpha that I learned to accept God's love and believed it was for me. Not just other people, but me too.

### How the World Defined Me

Who we are and the way we think about ourselves becomes central to our earthly identity. Day after day the things we say to ourselves and what we allow others to say about us become our internal affirmations. In other words, our identity is influenced by what we allow it to be influenced by. If it is our friends, then we care deeply about what our friends say about us. If it's our career, then we care deeply about the next promotion, or the title or value of our impact at work. Perhaps it's money—then we care a lot about how big our paycheck is and what we can buy. If it's material things, then the labels we wear, the handbags we carry, and the type of car we drive may matter a lot. The harsh truth is, we seek value and fulfillment from others that we can only get from God.

In that same vein, if Christ is central in our identity, then we allow our identity to be rooted in what Jesus says about us. Choosing to follow Jesus allows us to no longer put our identity in our positions, personalities, Enneagram numbers, what our family says, or our labels (friend, daughter, wife, sister, etc.). It allows us to put our identity in Jesus, Who says we are born of purpose, adopted into His family, accepted, chosen, predestined, redeemed, forgiven, planned for, sealed, blessed, and beloved. Biblical identity is different from what the world says we are. And that was something I did not understand—not a bit.

Up until that point in my life, I had let everything *but* God define me. I let the things people said about me define me: unwanted, an accident, ugly, not good enough, not strong enough, below average, and unnecessary. That my smile was too big and my thigh gap too small. That I worked too much and wasn't doing enough for my kids. That I was too timid or too professional. I let my roles define me: leader, mother, wife, friend, daughter, sister-in-law. I strived to be the best I could in each of the roles and never felt like I was good enough at any of them.

But don't you see? *Your identity cannot be achieved.* You cannot achieve some end point, some goal post, some finish line in any of our earthly roles. There is no "done."

There is no "perfect." Are you ever done being a mother? No. Is there a perfect mother? No. Are you ever done being a friend? No. You get the point. The reason I was not ful-filled was because there was no end to the work to be done in the roles or truth to the things said about me. Yet I acted and believed that there were. My guess is, you have done the same. We're all guilty of striving for the unachievable and thus letting these earthly identities become our truth. What on earth are we striving for?

**Drawing Near to God**

The dramatic shift I felt during the ten weeks of the Alpha course was like one big microwave moment. My whole world perspective had changed. However, I still had hang-ups and difficult emotions to work through as a re-sult of my adoption. While I did believe God loved me, I still struggled with the idea that He was the perfect Father. What did that mean? Since my own dad had passed away when I was nineteen, I had been living without a father in my life for nearly fourteen years. Reconciling the difference between an earthly father and a heavenly Father was chal-lenging. However, as challenging as it was, Paul was very clear in Romans 8:15 (NIV) when he wrote, "The Spirit you received does not make you slaves, so that you live in fear again; rather, the Spirit you received brought about your adoption to sonship. And by him we cry, 'Abba, Father.'"

Because we receive Jesus as our Savior, we no longer have to live a life without a perfect parent, because, as Paul further wrote in Ephesians 2, by receiving God, we have become adopted by God and made His heirs. It is because of this adoption that we have the right and the privilege to call God our Dad, Abba. In the original Hebrew, *Abba* is an intimate word for *father*, much like the word *daddy* in modern-day English. Because we are God's kids, we are able to refer to God in this intimate way, as a part of our relationship with Him.

I allowed these new-to-me truths about God as my heavenly Father start to replace the opinions, statements, and judgments from others. I recognized moments of seemingly micro-level clarity, where things started to build on each other. The more I read about God and what God said about me, the more I believed it. It did not happen overnight, and there were ups and downs. But, slowly starting when I finished Alpha in June 2014, the way I viewed myself through the eyes of God changed dramatically. We became regular church attendees, and my children began attending youth programs. It is because of this process, drawing near to God through prayer and through reading His Word, that I finally began to understand *and* accept that God loved me, for me. It did not happen instantly but grew with each faithful step. The biggest difficulty I faced was feeling worthy of God's love and letting go of the past hurts from years of not feeling good enough.

**Worthy**

If you're adopted or have simply been told you're not enough, perhaps you know exactly what I mean. If you ever lost a game or failed a test, or perhaps lost a friend, or have been left out, maybe you've felt this way too. As hard as it is to grasp, remember, you too are worthy of God's love.

You too are worthy of having a perfect parent—the only perfect parent—God. *You are worth more than what others say about you.*

The Enemy wants us to believe the lies others tell us about ourselves. He wants us to believe we are unworthy of being accepted, unworthy of love, unworthy of purpose, and unworthy of serving God. As an adoptee, these feelings are amplified. If unwanted or unplanned for, how could I possibly be worthy of being loved by God or of serving God? If not intentionally created by my parents, how could I possibly be qualified to serve God with intention?

The Enemy inserts these lies into our minds and sets us up for failure. When we believe these lies, we disqualify ourselves from serving because he casts fear into our hearts and tells us we are not good enough. As we choose to believe these lies, we step out of the light of God's path for us. We decide we are unworthy. However, when we truly believe and accept that we have a perfect Father Who loves us unconditionally and we are worthy of His love, we can break free of the chains of our past and live life truly loved. I knew this intellectually. I had read it dozens of times. I had heard it in sermons and in Bible studies.

But I didn't believe it was for me.

I knew it and believed it for other people.

But not for me.

The problem with this was rooted in my own rejection of God's love for me. For we are all called to accept God's good and perfect love for us, regardless of what other people say. Regardless of what we think and regardless of how we feel. This separation, this distance between me and my acceptance of God's love for me, was keeping me from living a life truly loved. We don't have to be good enough or perfect enough or be the best wife or mother, get the right promotion, or be thin enough to earn God's love. *There is nothing to earn.* God's love is freely available to us. All we must do is love Him and accept His love for us.

As the book of John proclaims, "But to all who believed him and accepted him, he gave the right to become children of God" (John 1:12 NLT). The core issue here is that I did not fully accept God. By not believing I was worthy of God's good and perfect love for me, I wasn't fully accepting God in my life. I wasn't making Him number one. I was still putting other things—specifically, acceptance by others, love by others, and achievement—ahead of accepting love from God. I was rejecting Him. I was sinning against God.

I was worthy of God's love.

But I was not accepting His love.

We are all worthy of God's love for us, not because of who we are or what we have done but because of Whose we are and Who He is. We can know this intellectually and still not believe it. You have to know it *and* believe it is for you. First John 4:10 (CSB) says, "Love consists in this: not that we loved God, but that he loved us and sent his Son to be the atoning sacrifice for our sins." Is there a greater love than this? To send your own son to sacrifice for all of us? Hear me. God's love is for you. It is for me. No one's opinions, no acts, nothing you are or do can earn this love. We only have to accept it.

Even though my birth parents put me up for adoption.

Even if you are adopted too.

Even if others say you are unwanted.

Even if you aren't perfect.

Even if you got pregnant.

Even if you can't.

Even if you haven't achieved your dreams.

God's love is for you, and it's for me too.

You don't have to live a life subject to your circumstances or feeling rejected, unaccepted, or ashamed. You don't have to live a life feeling less than or second best. You can choose to believe this truth: *God chose you, and you can decide to start living like it.* You can start living life adopted by the creator of the universe.

## Walking with God

In June 2017, things came to a head. I had worked through so many questions and had grown to love the Lord at a level I hadn't known possible in just three short years. I was finally in a place where I was spending daily time with God, in a relationship with Him, reading the Bible, praying regularly, and following the nudges He was giving me. One night I curled up in my bed, cuddled into my fuzzy blanket, and closed my eyes tight to pray.

I had come to realize that in order to know our purpose in life, we must know what's important to us, but in order to know what's important to us, we must know ourselves. However, to truly know ourselves, we must know our Creator—we must know God. To know God, we must spend time with God, build a relationship with Him, know His Word, know His character, spend time with Him in prayer, discern His direction for us, and then *follow through*. Only then will we be walking in God's purpose for us in His truth for our lives.

We won't do this perfectly, because we are all sinners, and as sinners we have sinful desires and sinful natures. We want to take control and do things on our own. The further away from God we are, the more likely we are to follow our own plans instead of the plans God has for us. When we stay close to God and walk with God in our day-to-day lives, we follow His direction, His nudges, and only then are we living out His purpose. The purpose He has for each and every one of us. The only way to have this awareness is to follow God's plan day by day.

I had been holding on to some control over my path and desire to find my birth parents. While the intent had been good, I was trying to do well across all facets of my life: work, motherhood, wife, daughter, and the list goes on. I had come to realize that I wasn't just trying to do well in those areas—I was defining myself and my identity through those roles. I had held on to finding my birth parents to define my own identity instead of releasing my identity to God first and to my birth parents and all the roles I was playing second. It was time to surrender. For Jesus said in Matthew 10:38, "And whoever does not take his cross and follow me, is not worthy of me." I was holding on to my own cross, idolizing my own achievements, my own roles, and my own life, where I called the shots. I knew to live a life where God was in control. I needed to submit to Him and His plan. I prayed this transformational prayer:

*God*, I am yours. I am no longer going to define my life by the roles I play or the different hats I wear. I will only define myself in the way You intended, as Your child. Perfect in Your eyes, no matter what I do or don't do. I know that no matter what happens, no matter what other people think or say or do to me, I can trust that my life is intentional, made with purpose and for You. Lord, if it is Your will, let me find my birth parents. No longer because they have or will define who I am but because I want to thank them for what they did—surrendering me to this life. Use this for your purpose. I surrender this to You. Amen.

## Reflection

*Questions*

1. How would you describe your identity? How might others describe you?
2. How would God describe you? How might that be different from how you or others would describe you?
3. Why is that distinction (you versus others versus God) important? Which matters most to you and why?

*Affirmations*

1. I am a part of God's family.
2. I have direct access to God because of Jesus.
3. Jesus died for me.

## chapter five

# NUDGES

*You did not choose me, but I chose you and*
*appointed you that you should go and bear*
*fruit and that your fruit should abide, so that*
*whatever you ask in my name, he may give*
*to you.*

John 15:16

A FEW DAYS AFTER MY PRAYER of surrender, I left for a
weekend away in Ohio with some close friends. Lau-
ren was pregnant with her first child, and we were reuniting
to attend her baby shower. I cashed in some hard-earned
travel points from countless business trips and booked a
fancy hotel for me and my friend Drea. Drea was also a
working mama, and we both needed a break from reality.
Since we were traveling out of state and arriving early, we
had the gift of time to spend catching up. In the weeks

leading up to the trip, we decided we would try to squeeze in a quick trip to a local spa the morning of the shower. The problem was we could not find one with availability. After numerous calls, somehow Drea found a place across town at another hotel and was able to book us.

We counted down the days to our girls' trip, and finally the day arrived. The morning of July 7, 2017, I took an early flight from Des Moines to Chicago, where I would meet up with Drea so we could fly together to Columbus. Arriving at O'Hare Airport on a busy Friday morning, Drea and I had coordinated a ninety-minute layover. That gave us just enough time to catch up over a quick bite to eat and catch our next flight. Since I arrived first, I found a quiet restaurant and settled in place at the bar. Drea showed up just moments later, and after a huge hug we sat down to order lunch.

When we were about halfway through our drinks, our phones buzzed with notifications that our flight had been canceled. Not delayed, canceled. After a few moments of panic, we received a second notice that our airline had rebooked us quickly, and thankfully we were on the next flight to Columbus just a few hours later. Since we had time, we snuck in a quick manicure at the airport spa, bonding over our kids' latest shenanigans. It felt so good to sit in this space, connecting with Drea after a few years apart and simply resting in the moment.

The rest of the trip into Columbus and throughout the whole evening, Drea and I talked nonstop. I shared my recent feelings about my birth parents. She was so understanding and gentle with my raw emotions. I couldn't tell you what time we finally went to sleep that night, but I do remember I felt more loved and supported in this place of unknown than I had in a long, long time.

The next morning, Drea and I walked to the nearest Starbucks, enjoyed breakfast, and then went back to the hotel to get ready for our friend's baby shower. I felt a bit unsettled all morning and couldn't quite shake it. I kept thinking about the conversation Drea and I had the previous night and the prayers I had made a few days before. I was thinking about the unsettled feeling while taking a shower, wrestling with it and trying to peel back the layers to discover what was causing it. Running through the options: Was it work? No. Was it the kids? No. What was lingering, open ended? As soon as I paused, it struck me.

The stirring was the desire to find my birth parents. It was back.

A little shiver ran down my spine.

Somehow, this time it felt different. Instead of consuming thoughts, I felt much calmer and more collected. I pushed the feelings aside, knowing I didn't have time to sit with them today—at least, not right then.

### Turning Point

We arrived at the spa and checked in. Drea was getting a pedicure, and I was getting a massage. The rush of traveling to Columbus, the delayed flights, and the deep conversation from the prior night all caught up with me the moment I lay down for the massage. A rush of exhaustion hit me, and I found myself emotional but couldn't put my finger on why. As the hour passed, I found myself thinking about my family, and I choked back a few tears. I was so thankful God gave me this sweet, slow moment, this trip, to recharge, rest, and relax. I loved my family more than anything, but I needed this time to think. There was something special about it—there was a reason we were here.

I stepped into the light of the open spa and sat with Drea while she finished getting her nails done. The woman in the pedicure chair next to her flipped through a magazine. The two nail technicians were discussing (not so quietly) a friend they had in common. I was trying to tune them out while I exchanged some text messages with my husband about the kids back at home. As they were talking, I could feel Drea's eyes looking at me—*no*—staring at me. I looked up at her. She had one eyebrow raised and mouthed, *Are you listening?*

I shook my head that I wasn't, but I started paying attention.

The two women were discussing some recent drama with their mutual friend. From what I could gather, their friend had recently found out that her father wasn't really her father after taking a DNA test offered by some website. As I listened more closely, I learned that the woman had taken a DNA test on Ancestry.com out of curiosity to find out more about her heritage.

*That's interesting*, I thought. *I have never been able to answer questions about my ethnicity before. That's definitely something I would be interested in knowing.*

For a moment, I fantasized about what it would be like to be able to answer the simple question of "What's your ethnicity?" something I had never been able to respond to. Unless "American" counts. I really had no idea. I realized I had lost track of the conversation and turned back to listen again.

"So she opens up her results, and get this—not only is she not Spanish like she thought she was, but she is a match to people that she has no idea who they are! Can you believe it?" the first woman says.

"Wait, what? What does that mean?" the second woman questioned.

"Well, what happened is, after she started going through them, she realizes none of the people on the list match up with her dad . . . and finally figures out that the dad she knew her whole life wasn't actually her dad after all. Her mom had been lying to her for over twenty years!"

"Woah . . . all that from a simple DNA test?" the second woman asked.

"Yup. Crazy, right?"

I stared at Drea, my mind racing. I had never heard of this test before or knew anything about it, but it sounded like not only could it give ethnicity information but also matched you with actual real relatives. Could that test be the answer to some of my lifelong questions about who I was? Could I really get the answer about my ethnicity or where I came from? Would I find people I was related to? What would it be like to be able to say, oh yeah, I'm actually English or German or . . . anything, with real confidence?

Drea and I were locked in this stare for what felt like minutes. It could have just been seconds, but it felt like a long time. I had been eavesdropping for long enough, and I spoke up. "What did you say the name of this site was?"

"Ancestry.com or something like that," the first woman said.

Without hesitation or thought, I acted. I pulled open my phone and scrolled to the web browser icon. The default landing page opened, and I typed *Ancestry.com* into the search bar and hit Go.

The next few moments felt as if they were taking place in slow motion—through a fog. Without hesitation, I reached for my phone, typed in my password to unlock the screen, and navigated to the internet browser. I slowly typed *AncestryDNA Kit* in the search bar and hit Return. Time seemed to stand still as the search results loaded. One of the first links that popped up said *Join the world's largest consumer DNA database & discover your ethnic mix today! Safe and secure. Simple and easy. Ethnicity mix, report, family history.*

"Family history . . ." I mumbled. Interesting. The next link was *How AncestryDNA works.*

I clicked.

My heart started to beat faster as I read the page that loaded next.

*Six million people have learned more about themselves. Are you next? The largest DNA network in the world helped more people find their story in their DNA. Discover yours— and learn who your ancestors were and where they came from.*

Wow.

I read through the statement on the screen again. *Discover yours . . . learn your ancestors . . .* Could this . . . could this give me some information I was missing? Could one simple test tell me who I was? Was it possible that I could, for the first time, be able to answer a basic question about my ethnicity? That would be . . . fulfilling.

I kept scrolling.

*Nigerian? Sicilian? What are you?*

Great question! I smirked at the joke in my head. I kept scrolling.

*Who are your people? Connect with living relatives who share parts of your DNA—and use 90 million Ancestry family trees to fill in pieces of your family history.*

Wait. Living relatives? Maybe I would be able to find a distant cousin or someone to help narrow down the search. Even a small clue could make a huge difference, given I had failed to make any traction in the past.

I clicked again.

Without thinking about what I was doing, I felt an overwhelming urge to move forward. It might have been a newer development, recognizing these nudges, these little stirrings in my heart, but I knew what that feeling was. It was God. I knew it was God because there's no way I would do what I was about to do out of my own desire. I was now in my own little world, smiling at my phone, understanding now it was no mistake we had ended up where we were today. That this was the only spa available—inconveniently on the other side of town. God had a plan. A plan for me to hear about this, this option. To find out more about who I was. Despite the significance of what I was doing, I felt completely and overwhelming calm, yet another sign that God was with me in the moment. I clicked a few more times, entered my PayPal information, and before I really processed what I was doing, I had ordered an Ancestry-DNA kit.

I sat back in my seat, completely unaware of anything happening around me. I looked up and noticed that Drea was smiling in my direction. Drea knew I had searched for my birth family on and off for years without any success. She knew I had accepted where I was but longed to understand the medical history I was passing down to my kids, and most importantly, the desire to thank my parents for the loving sacrifice they had made in giving me a better life. She knew the significance of the conversation we had just overheard together. And she saw me go into my own shell after hearing it.

As we were walking out of the spa, Drea turned to me, raised one eyebrow, and asked, "So did you buy it?"

"Yep."

"Good." And with that, we left.

## Follow-Through

After I had been home from Ohio a few days, the kit arrived. It came in a small, shrink-wrapped white box no bigger than two decks of cards. David brought it into the house and laid it on the island in the kitchen.

"Are you going to take that?" he asked, matter of fact. He knew what had been on my heart.

I hesitated. "I'm not sure." In the days since I had ordered the kit, my mind had raced. I second-guessed myself. What was I thinking? Taking a DNA test seemed . . . final. If my DNA was out there, could others find me too? What if it was a bad situation? What if I actually *did* find relatives? And what if that was a door I couldn't shut? But then on the flip side, what if it was actually good? What if I could find out where I came from? What if I could thank them for what they did? Not only would I get answers to the medical information I had started out wondering and searching about, but also answers to ethnicity, who I was, where I came from, and maybe, just maybe, I could learn who they were. I could learn more about where I came from and what made me, me.

However, a part of me was nervous about what I might find. Aside from the medical and ethnicity questions, what if they were dead? Or in jail? My mom would probably be super upset when she found out I did it, but she was the one who'd started this—she'd told me to go find the letter. This was the means to that end.

By the time the kit arrived, I'd thought I would have the kit on hand and then could take whatever time I needed to decide if I wanted to take the DNA test. This would give me plenty of time to think through all the possible outcomes and then decide about sending it in. After spending a decade as an auditor, my mind was wired to think of possible outcomes from a given scenario. I needed time. Time to think through all the options, all the possibilities that could come from this test and its results. I hadn't prayed about it and was wrestling with this on my own.

David stared at me. "Just take it."

"I'm not ready to do that. I just need time to think." I looked down and then back up at him. He knew me better than anyone. Knew all I had been through, all that I had wondered.

"I've known you for over a decade, Wendy. I know you've been thinking about this, probably endlessly. You've been trying to find answers for over seven years. Just take the test."

The box sat on our counter for a few days. Unmoved. My husband continued to urge me to just go for it.

Finally I felt the nudge. In a moment of uncharacteristic action, I ripped the shrink-wrap off and opened the box. I did not think. I did not so much as feel. I leaned into the nudge and acted. The whole thing felt like an out-of-body experience.

I stood there over the bathroom sink, looking at the test tube. Out of the corner of my eye, I could see myself in the mirror. My mind was blank. No thoughts. Just looking at it. After several moments, I took the test, then put the test in the packaging, sealed the box, and affixed the label. I held the results in my hand. The whole thing felt so surreal.

What could come of this? What answers might be in this tiny tube of saliva? Would it be good news? Or bad? Or perhaps no news at all?

I set it on the cool counter.

And waited.

Two more days passed with the box sitting still, unmoved, on our bathroom counter.

Again, David urged me to mail it.

And in a rare moment of blind faith, I did.

## Reflection

*Questions*

1. Do you feel like you have a purpose in life? If so, what is it? If not, how might you explore this with God?

2. Have you ever felt like you should do something but didn't know why? Thinking back now, could those nudges be from God? Why or why not?

3. What is holding you back from drawing near to God? Why?

*Affirmations*
1. When I draw near to God, God draws near to me.
2. God chose me.
3. God wants to be in a relationship with me.

*chapter six*

### GOD'S TIMELINE

*"For I know the plans I have for you," says the*
*Lord. "They are plans for good and not for*
*disaster, to give you a future and a hope. In those*
*days when you pray, I will listen. If you look for*
*me wholeheartedly, you will find me."*
Jeremiah 29:11–13 NLT

TWO WEEKS LATER WE PACKED UP the kids and were headed on a twelve-hour drive to Colorado to spend a few days with family before my sister-in-law's wedding. As we pulled out of the driveway, I asked David to stop. Reaching into my bag, I lifted out an envelope I had been carrying around since the time I'd mailed my Ancestry-DNA test. The envelope contained a single-page form, submitting information I knew about myself and my adoption to the International Soundex Reunion Registry, a free service. The registry service is a nonprofit organization that allows adoptees and other family members to submit information, and if mutually submitted and a match is made, both parties are notified of a match. This was a long shot, but after stewing over it and carrying the form around for a few weeks, I felt the nudge to finally mail it.

I climbed back into the car, and we started the drive.

Curled up in the passenger seat, while the kids were content, I alternated between reading and staring out the window most of the drive. I thought about the DNA test obsessively. According to the information on the Ancestry website, the test normally takes eight weeks to process and another four weeks for results to be compiled. I assumed that meant I had about twelve weeks to process my thoughts and emotions related to any possible outcome.

I started thinking through the possible outcomes, turning each one over slowly, as if studying a new rock or pebble for the first time. I explored each possibility and felt what each outcome might be like. It certainly wasn't the first time I had fantasized about my birth parents, but this time felt different. The idea of identifying them, knowing who they were and what had happened to them, was suddenly a real possibility. Who knew how long it could take, but this search, this time, felt different.

I had recently joined a Facebook group called DNA Detectives, looking for resources on what to do with DNA once I had received it. For the last few weeks, I watched other stories being told by other adoptees searching for their families. Adoptees and birth parents were a part of the group, and this gave me a new perspective about what the birth-parent experience might be like. As one might expect, the results were all over the board. Some adoptees never found their birth parents. Some found their birth parents, only to learn their birth parents wanted nothing to do with them, thus, opening a deep wound of rejection for a second time (once at birth and again at reunion). This was a real possibility for me too. I had been told my birth mother had wanted to put me up for adoption, that she'd wanted to give me a better life, so perhaps she wouldn't want to connect with me. I also was told my birth father was not involved, so my guess was he definitely wouldn't want to connect with me.

Of course, there were worse possibilities as well. My birth parents could be deceased. I had already lost a parent (my father) and didn't know what it might feel like to potentially have lost one or both of my birth parents as well. Doing some quick math, I realized my birth parents would be about fifty years old, so the possibility they were living was pretty good. Then there was always the chance they could be incarcerated or have criminal backgrounds, which would also be tricky to navigate. What then?

I kept my expectations low and my hope tempered. But I would be fooling myself to dismiss the fact that there was a possibility that I, too, like so many of the success stories within the DNA Detectives group, could *actually* find my birth parents and it *could* be a happy ending. Seeing so many cases of reunion gave me a glimmer of hope that I could find them and that it was truly possible to connect with them. A hope I so clearly realized I'd had all along. I had pushed it so deep, hoping not to be hurt, hoping not to be rejected. But it was there, and for the first time in my life, I was willing to let it grow.

As I spent more time with DNA Detectives, I learned

the group contained several people designated as "Search Angels." The search angels were trained in reviewing DNA and/or other family information alongside available records to connect adoptees and birth parents, siblings, and other family members. I passively watched them reunite others in the group with success.

That day, on our drive to Colorado, I wrote my first post asking for help to find my birth parents. Hoping a search angel would be willing to help me too.

**Matches**

We had arrived in Fort Collins after the long drive late that night. We were staying at a boutique hotel in which every room was renovated differently. The next day we spent time with our family and celebrated my sister-in-law and her groom-to-be at the rehearsal dinner. It was such an exciting few days, and while so thrilled for her and her partner, the pending test results and my search lingered in the back of my mind at all times. Day three in Colorado was the wedding day and marked just two weeks since my DNA kit was received by Ancestry for processing. Although the timeline was an eight-week processing time, followed by four weeks of compounding the results, a small part of me wondered if the information might come sooner. As I lay down the night before the wedding, I thought it would be just my luck if results came in the morning, and I was stranded in the mountains without cell service to look at anything—the hotel had cell service, but not the wedding venue.

The next morning I blinked open my eyes to the sound of raindrops hitting the window. Today was the day! My sister-in-law's wedding day, and there was a lot to do to get everyone ready. Not only was I her bridesmaid, but my daughter was the flower girl and my son was the ring bearer. I reached for my phone on the rickety nightstand and punched in my passcode. I checked my email with one eye open and scrolled through, deleting the junk mail and skimming for anything needing attention. I stopped suddenly and gasped.

There it was.

An email from Ancestry.com.

My results were ready.

God has such a sense of humor. *Of course* they came today. *Of course* I'd had that now not-so-hilarious thought last night. *Of course* I wouldn't have time to pore over them today. I laughed out loud.

Everyone else was still asleep, so I curled up under the covers, in the dim light of the morning, and tapped the email. I was prompted to open up the web page and log in to my account.

I had matches. Lots of them—literally hundreds of matches. I reached for my glasses on the nightstand and put them on so I could see more clearly. I clicked the View All DNA Matches button in bright-blue lettering to see what might be there. A huge list popped up, separated by segments of *Close Family, 1st Cousin, 2nd Cousin, 3rd Cousin,* and so on.

I froze.

I had two matches under *Close Family.* I threw off the covers and sat up straight in bed. Who needed coffee when you'd just found blood relatives for the first time in your life?

I stared at the two user names. Names I had never heard before. Sitting right there was close-family DNA matches. I clicked around looking for what *Close Family* meant. Were these aunts, uncles, grandparents, or could they be my birth parents? Next to each name was a statement on shared DNA, which explained how much DNA you shared with that particular person.

I knew I had seen a chart somewhere that explained, for each family relationship, how much shared DNA existed in a range. I racked my brain. Where had I seen that before?

Oh! I threw the covers off and put my feet on the cold wooden floorboards. I shrugged my bathrobe on and went into the bathroom and shut the door. I needed light, and I didn't want to wake up my kids yet. I checked the clock, trying to figure out how long I could dig into this before I absolutely *had* to get my family up and moving for the day's festivities.

I scrolled through my pictures thinking I might have saved the DNA chart to photos. Not there. Where was it? Ah! In that Facebook group—DNA Detectives. I flipped to my Facebook app and went into the group and then to the files. I found the chart, pulled it up, and started to interpret it. The chart, titled "DNA Detectives Autosomal Statistics Chart," was divided into groups. Each group represented a set of potential relationships. I flipped back to my matches. The top two matches shared 1600 to 1850 centimorgans, which matched up on the chart to the half sibling, aunt/uncle/niece/nephew, or grandparent-grandchild—Group B.

I gasped. *That's really close!* The only other closer

matches were listed as full sibling or parent-child relationships. Apparently, I was loud, because my husband mumbled, "What's going on," still half-asleep.

"I HAVE MATCHES!" I said in the least quiet whisper.

I sat down on the edge of the bed and showed him what I had found.

It was clear based on the user ID of my first match that the last name of the individual was most likely Lindberg. Although not super common, it was also not super uncommon. That might be a good lead. I scanned photos where I had saved a class list from 1985, which I had found a couple of weeks ago. That would've been the graduating year of my birth mom. I looked for a last name of Lindberg, but I didn't find one. Certainly there were lots of reasons why that could be the case. It could actually be a name on my birth father's side. It could be a married name instead of a maiden name. Who knew. The list could also be incomplete, given that I did find it by googling it. A better source would've been a high school yearbook, something I had considered finding several years ago. *It might just be time to find that now.*

I didn't know for sure, but I did wonder if my birth father might have gone to high school with my birth mother. It would make a lot of sense that they would know each other through school. Or, perhaps a neighboring school, given my parents and I had lived in a metro area with several high schools within the district. The other user ID was made up of letters and numbers that appeared to be some sort of initials and perhaps a date. Either way, I was running short on time, and I was certainly not going to figure this out while holing up in the bathroom on a single morning. This was going to take more investigative work.

But I did know this for certain—these two individuals, my closest matches, were directly related to my birth parents. And that was far closer than I ever expected to match right out of the gate. How amazing that God immediately gave me those answers. How on earth was I going to focus the rest of the day?

## Knowing God versus Knowing about God

There is a big difference between knowing someone and knowing about them. Consider the difference in reading a book about your spouse versus actually knowing them, loving them, and being in relationship with them. These are two different things. Up until this point, I only knew basic information about my birth parents. And even then it was only a set of facts that neatly fit on one sheet of paper, along with a few things my mom remembered about my birth mother from the attorney. Knowing about them without any context, knowing about their personalities, their life stories, their interests, what they did in their lives, or who they really were, meant that I really didn't know them. I only knew a small sliver about them.

Likewise there's a big difference between knowing about God and knowing God. You may know about God and know He created the universe. You may know He sent His son, Jesus, to die for your sins. But in the same way knowing about my birth parents and knowing my birth parents are different things, knowing about God and knowing God, *really knowing Him*, are also very different. Reading about God and what He's done in the Bible isn't enough. We can be biblically deep and relationally shallow. We also need to have a relationship with the Lord. James 4:8 says, "Draw near to God, and he will draw near to you." When we engage in a daily walk with God, praying with Him, listening to Him, and responding, we are deepening our relationship with the Lord. We are knowing *Him*, not just knowing about Him.

Ironically, when I was growing closer to God, not just in knowing about Him through Alpha, but really growing in my relationship with Him, my desires evolved too. When I surrendered my desire for God's plans, my desire to learn about my birth parents, my ethnicity, and my origin evolved. I realized in this moment that I wanted to know my birth parents. It is not lost on me that these two things happened about the same time.

**Wedding Day**

After getting everyone ready, fed, and loaded into the car, we trekked up the mountain. My sister-in-law had selected an outdoor venue that backed up to a beautiful river. The only challenge was no cell service. On the way up the mountain, I did as much digging as I could until the service dropped. I started by going back to my original DNA results and looking, for the first time, at the ethnicity portion. Ironic, because that was something I was very interested in, and the reason I sent the DNA test in the first place was to learn about my ethnicity—and yet this was the last place I looked once the results arrived.

So that day, August 3, 2017, I could for the first time answer the question, Who are you?

If you're not adopted, this may not seem so significant. But if you are adopted like me, this may be a pain point for you. A simple question about national heritage for a school project, such as a report on your ancestors, becomes difficult when you have no idea who they are. It can become a painful reminder that you simply don't know where you came from, you don't know who your parents are, and there's a hole in your history—and no matter how much you want to, you just can't fill it.

Well, that day I could fill that hole.

As the hairstylist my sister-in-law had hired for us for the wedding started to brush out my hair, which is long and dark, she said, "Wow! You have really beautiful hair," then asked, "What's your ethnic background? It's so dark!"

Again, God, with His sense of humor, giving me an opportunity just moments later to answer this question I had wondered about and wanted to answer my whole life.

"Norwegian, Swedish, German, and Czech, primarily," I answered, grinning from ear to ear. It felt so . . . peaceful . . . so easy . . . to be able to answer that question. I felt . . . normal. Like I belonged. I finally knew a piece of my own history that I had longed to know for my entire life.

And that was just the beginning.

## Reflection

*Questions*

1. Can you think of times where things did not work out when you wanted them to?
2. Looking back now, can you see how God moved to make things happen at the right time?
3. How has God's timing impacted your life?

*Affirmations*
1. God's plan is perfect.
2. God's timing is trustworthy.
3. I fit into God's grand plan for the world.

*chapter seven*

## TRUSTING GOD

> *Trust in the Lord with all your heart, and do*
> *not lean on your own understanding. In all*
> *your ways acknowledge him, and he will make*
> *straight your paths.*
> Proverbs 3:5–6

THE REST OF THE WEEKEND WAS a blur. After a wonderful time with family, celebrating my sister-in-law, a few too many ice cream sundaes, and one delicious brunch, we loaded back into the car and headed east back home to Des Moines. David was so sweet to drive almost the whole way back so I could spend time trying to find more information digging through the DNA results. The weekend had been so busy with celebrations, I hadn't been able to search for any additional information.

As soon as we merged onto the interstate, I sent three messages through Ancestry.com to my top three matches. I had read on the DNA Detectives Facebook group on how to approach someone with matching DNA, to not be too abrasive or alarming, and went with generic messages. Of the top three matches, two were classified as "close relative," and the one that classified as "1st cousin" appeared to be directly related to one of the close relative matches.

The message I sent: "Hello! I recently submitted my DNA to Ancestry, and it came back with a match for us. I would like to connect with you to determine how we might be related." None of these accounts appeared to have recent logins, so I didn't expect to get responses anytime soon.

I leaned back in my seat and exhaled. My shoulders sank, and I realized I had been holding tension in my shoulders to the point that they were approaching my ears. I guess it was safe to say I was nervous.

"This doesn't feel real," I said to David.

He looked at me from across the front seat and smiled. "Now we wait, right?"

"Well, sort of. I think I can keep digging into the other information and see if it relates at all to the matches. Who knows—these people may not check Ancestry often at all. We may never hear from them."

I sat quietly for a few minutes, processing. There was more to do. I hadn't really searched any of Ancestry's documents. I had both my birth parents' birth dates. I wondered if maybe I could come up with some sort of population of people who might have those birth dates. I clicked around on the website for a few minutes and quickly found a promising Search function. I searched on the site's Birth, Marriage, and Death Record Index for my birth parents' birthdates. From my information sheet, I knew not just their birthdays but the state they were born in, their hair and eye colors, along with height and weight. No names of course, but this information might get me started. I'd had this information since I'd collected the envelope of adoption records from my mother, but for some reason I had never searched this data in the Ancestry database. It was as if I was seeing this information and this path for the first time.

I searched my birth mother's information first. I typed in her birth date and state of birth, Illinois. Several birth records popped up, but no Illinois. I quickly googled to see if Illinois birth records were public information and learned, unfortunately, they were not. A dead end.

Based on what I had read in several forums and groups, it sounded like birth fathers were less likely to be responsive. My expectations were low, but I decided to search his birth date anyway. I typed in my birth father's birth date and his state of birth, Texas. I checked the box for *Exact* so my results would be to the specific date entered, helping me narrow down results. I figured I could always go and expand that later, but this would at least get me started. I hit Search.

The initial results came back with 231,698 records. *Wow, that's a lot of records.* I scrolled through the screens of link after link, interpreting what was coming up. It looked like I could narrow the results further by selecting a sub-list of the results to just "Birth, Baptism & Christening" records. I clicked the link to narrow the search, and a new screen appeared. Now 216,665 records. *Great. That's not very helpful.* But again I saw there was an option to narrow the results further. I clicked the link to select "Birth, Baptism & Christening" under "All Texas Birth Index 1903–1997," and a new screen appeared yet again.

The results narrowed dramatically.

Down to 328.

This seemed like I might be on to something, so I pulled out my laptop. It was time to build a spreadsheet. This was a manageable number that was actually worth narrowing down, even if it meant digging into each and every one of those 328 results. I turned on my hotspot and regenerated the same query over again to both confirm it was the right results and to ensure I had a live list I could export into Excel. Sure enough, same list appeared. This felt like a real lead. My heart was fluttering, and I could feel my neck turning red. I turned to David and explained what I had found.

"This is really promising," I said. "I am sure we can narrow it down from here." I kept going. I felt like we were moving through slow motion, yet I kept moving forward.

I exported the list into an Excel workbook. The export gave me links to the actual birth records, the name of the individual (first, middle, and last names), the birth date, the birth county, the father's and mother's first, middle, and last names. That was a lot of information! I retyped the data into an easier-to-read and easier-to-search format. A few hours into the drive, and I had a list. Once the spreadsheet was formatted, I combed for a class list from my birth mother's high school. This time for what would have been my birth father's graduating-class year. I didn't know if he went there, but I figured it was worth a shot. If I could find it, perhaps I could cross reference it with this birth-index information and look for a match. Either way, I knew my birth father was somewhere on that birth registry list. One of those 328 people was my birth father.

It took me about an hour of searching to track down a high school class list. It was from a website I didn't feel super confident in, but it was a class list I could try nonetheless. I typed up the list of names into a separate tab of my Excel workbook just in time for the sun to go down and my battery to nearly die, making it difficult to work on my laptop. The kids were hungry, so we stopped for dinner and watched a movie the rest of the way home. It was late and we were exhausted, so I'd pick up my search again in the morning.

## Analysis

The next morning, warm coffee in hand, I powered on my laptop, fully charged, picking up where I'd left off the day before. I built a formula to match the names between the birth-index export and the class-list export. It took me an hour to get my formula to work correctly. By comparing last names from the birth-records list and last names from the class list, it would flag any last name from the class list that also showed up on the birth registry. Several names popped up as matches due to last names being common, and I manually went through them one by one to confirm the first names were not matches.

I flipped through the rows and deleted the matches where there were false positives. There were five false positives.

Except one.

One name matched. First name and last name.

Exactly, one full name.

And *I recognized it.*

Lindberg.

The last name of this person was the same name in one of my close-family DNA matches. Lindberg. James Lindberg. Right there in clear black and white. All three sources lined up: the class list, the birth registry, and my DNA test. I couldn't believe it.

"David! I think I found him!" I rose from my desk and went to find him in the kitchen. "I found him."

"Really? Are you sure?"

"Yes, yes, I . . . I guess I am sure. I can't believe this. Come look."

All the doubt, all the second-guessing, all the concern that I wouldn't find him. It all disappeared in that instant. I felt a tremendous weight lift off me. I felt pounds lighter.

We wandered back to our office, and I walked him through my lists and showed him how I'd utilized the information on the Ancestry website. We agreed—it looked like a legitimate match worth exploring. I gave him the name, and he went to see if James Lindberg had a criminal record or any concerning background through the court system. With little ones, we wanted to be careful. We had agreed, if things looked concerning, we would proceed with an abundance of caution.

While David did some digging into the background, I turned to Facebook to find a way to track down more information about my presumed birth father. I started by searching *Lindberg.* Lots of results came up. Then I thought

I could try the name of the other match—the one related to the Lindberg name. That account had a first and last name for a user ID. I tried that name—Judith Shoolery.

Bingo.

Exactly one match came up. I clicked on her name to navigate to her Facebook profile. I clicked on Friends and scanned for any Lindbergs.

There were several.

And two named Jim Lindberg.

One appeared older and one younger.

I flipped back to the birth record I had found for James Lindberg on Ancestry just yesterday.

No. Freaking. Way.

The James Lindberg that matched my Ancestry birth registry and class list had a father named . . . James Lindberg.

I hadn't noticed that yesterday. This was just too obvious. It was right there under my nose.

This had to be them.

James Lindberg—my grandfather, and James Lindberg—my birth father.

A tingle started in my neck and ran down my spine and both my arms.

It was him. I knew it. I had not just found out who he was, but I found *him*. I found him, his father (my presumed biological paternal grandfather), and it appeared, based on his pictures, his kids. My siblings.

*My* siblings.

Stunned.

Speechless.

I leaned in and studied the picture closely. I couldn't believe my eyes, but there they were. Two younger kids, smiling back through the screen. They appeared much younger than me, which gave me pause. The last thing I wanted was to bother them or intrude in any way. I quickly decided that although it was shocking to see siblings for the first time, I would not ask my birth parents to meet or engage with any siblings I might have on either side. I was curious, of course, but I wasn't coming forward to pursue a relationship, and I definitely did not want to approach siblings who might or might not know that I existed. A relationship was not my goal. I wanted medical information and to know *about* them, and that could be accomplished with minimal interaction.

I did not expect my birth parents to want a relationship, because of their choice, and I respected that. Based on the information shared previously about my birth, I understood that this man, my birth father, was not involved in my birth, and thus, I did not expect him to be involved in my life now. All I wanted was some basic information, and if I could get that, that would be enough. Knowing who they were was a huge piece of my history that was on the verge of being solved, and hopefully I could get medical information from them directly. Beyond that . . . well, I didn't think there would be a beyond that.

I just hoped they could be reached.

## God Is Trustworthy

I'll admit it. Trusting people can be really hard. Depending on what has happened in your life, you might find it hard to trust people too. Trust can be especially difficult for adoptees because of underlying abandonment issues and the rejection from our births. Often in adoptions, the positive sides are highlighted: the unification of a baby with a wanting family. The joy of creating a family unit where one was absent before. However, there's another side to adoption. The birth parents.

As painful as it is to admit, for one family to be created by placing the baby with the adoptive parents, another family has to end. The birth parents are separated from that baby. Said another way, the birth parents are separated *from us*. In this moment, where I had identified who my presumed birth father was, I was confronted with the risk of being rejected again. That deep wound, the rejection that comes alongside an adoptee's journey, is not often discussed. No one likes to talk about that hardship because the feelings aren't so happy.

*But God.*

As I was sitting on that day, reading and poring over the details, thoughts of rejection and hurt came to the surface. When the rejection felt dark and heavy and I was sure no one could understand, God did. No one knows just how much I cried that day, but God does. He was there, making all broken things new. There were tears of joy, of nervousness, of decades of curiosity unfolding in front of me. Even though that rejection could be painful, I knew I could go through with it because I had the safety and security of *the* Father. God had accepted me no matter what happened next.

**Surrender**

I read everything I could read about Jim from his Facebook profile. I searched LinkedIn and read his profile there. My husband ran a background check. Everything matched up with what I knew about him. Location, age, everything. We concluded we had a substantial amount of information between the DNA match with his father, my presumed biological grandfather, his match to the class list, the birth registry, his Facebook profile, and LinkedIn timelines—everything matched. We had an abundance of information and had spent most of the day questioning it, cross-referencing it, and looking for holes in the research.

Everything lined up, and we felt confident we had what we needed to officially say yes, this man was my birth father.

As we sat back and looked at the information, all the files and profiles, we were both convinced this was it. It was shocking how quickly it came together, and we felt like we needed to check it over several times to be sure, but it was clear. God had provided an abundance of information in such a short time that we were shocked. Convinced, but shocked.

I took a screen shot of his picture and compared it to mine. We *did* look alike. This was definitely not our strongest evidence, but it put some reality to the situation. It put faces to names. It brought realness to the name I'd spent so much time analyzing and poring over. I stood in our bedroom, surrounded by printouts and information I had found, and I looked at this side-by-side comparison of a man who I was pretty sure was my birth father. A single tear dropped down my right cheek.

Because none of the research seemed unusual or concerning, and I felt peace with it, we decided together that if I wanted to, we were comfortable with initiating contact. I spent a couple of hours writing and rewriting a first message. There isn't really a guide on how to contact your birth parents for the first time, but I had searched and read several examples on the internet, and they all aligned on one thing: Don't be accusatory or pushy. Initiate contact and don't be too direct as to why.

This was it.

After what felt like a hundred edits, I finally crafted a message I felt like I could send.

> Jim,
> You don't know me, but I'm hoping you can help me—I recently took a DNA test and submitted it through Ancestry.com. I'm sure this is not the average Facebook message, and I understand if you would like to take some time to think about this before responding.
>
> It appears as though we might be related, based on what I can piece together through Facebook and Ancestry. Is it possible that you or a sibling of yours could have been born on May 25, 1965, in Texas, and gave a baby up for adoption in December of 1983? That information would be a match with the limited information I have regarding my biological father.
>
> Any information you could provide would be helpful. Thank you for your consideration. I hope to hear from you.
> Wendy

I prayed one last prayer: *Lord, I am putting all my trust in You. If this is Your will for me to contact this man, who, by all signs, all research, appears to be my birth father, please help me to know it is the right thing to do. I surrender this to You.*

My body tingled, starting in the back of my neck, across my shoulders, and down my arms. Okay, that was the sign I needed. *The Holy Spirit is with me, and I trust Him.* The goose bumps were followed by a sense of peace from head to toe. Feeling no reservations, and fully trusting Him, I hit Send.

## Reflection

*Questions*

1. Do you believe God is trustworthy? Why or why not?

2. Looking at your past, can you identify three to five times where God helped you get through a situation?

3. If God has helped you before, do you trust that He will again? Why or why not?

*Affirmations*

1. I can trust God's plan for me.
2. I can trust God is in the details of my life.
3. I matter to God.

# chapter eight

❦

## FOUND

*In him we have redemption through his
blood, the forgiveness of our trespasses, according
to the riches of his grace, which he lavished upon
us, in all wisdom and insight making known
to us the mystery of his will, according to his
purpose, which he set forth in Christ as a plan
for the fullness of time, to unite all things in him,
things in heaven and things on earth.*
Ephesians 1:7–10

IT WAS IMPOSSIBLE TO FOCUS THAT Monday. Not only
had I returned from our trip to Colorado to an inbox
full of emails to catch up on, but with this pending contact
to my birth father, and the deep desire to track down my
birth mother, focusing wasn't going well. Work crept by
one hour at a time. I raced home, ate dinner with my family, put my kids to bed, and immediately jumped back onto

the computer to continue digging. Any extra minute I had, I was trying to glue information together.

I kept coming back to the user name for the third match of my top three matches. It was a combination of letters and numbers that looked like initials followed by a date.

As I'd spent nearly ten years of my career as an auditor, dissecting information and looking for connectivity in details is something that comes somewhat naturally to me.

I started by googling the username, trying to find it on some other site or used in some other way in hopes that I could connect the user ID to an actual name, as I hadn't made any progress in figuring out my birth mother's side of the DNA results.

I searched and searched through pages of Google results with little success. I found one link that appeared to be a username on an old comment, a review of technology equipment, but I couldn't find any information about the person associated with that username. I might have hit a dead end. I felt like I had done everything I could on my own and had come up with no connections, no real leads. All I had been able to find all day was the class list from the year my birth mother would have graduated from Roosevelt High School.

The next day, Tuesday, I checked to see if Jim had read my Facebook message. He still hadn't. Trying to stay positive, I took that as a good thing. At least he hadn't read it and ignored it. I turned back to the DNA Detectives Facebook group in hopes of finding someone who might help me with my birth mother search. I had DNA matches, my birth mother's date of birth, location of birth, hair and eye color, what high school she went to, along with a class list, yet I couldn't figure out how to triangulate this information into any sort of list of potential birth parents. This was fairly frustrating for someone who was used to being able to look at data and figure out answers. I needed either a birth registry list from Illinois, where she was born, or to figure out more information about this connection from her side of my biological family. I knew I could figure it out if I just had one of those two things.

I started to draft a post for this Facebook group but kept getting interrupted throughout the day. It was midafternoon before I finally drafted a message I felt comfortable posting. I hit Post and then left to get a cup of coffee to help me make it through the rest of the afternoon.

By the time I returned to my desk fifteen minutes later, I had a message in my inbox from a woman who was a search angel. Her name was Christina Pearson, and she helped people find their relatives using DNA and genealogy. Christina was a genetic genealogist by trade and owned a small company called DNA Discoveries LLC. She helped people professionally as a part of her job but also helped people in this DNA Detectives Facebook group with small searches that didn't take much time. She took the information I had shared, and she started triangulating it with various databases she had access to. I ended up messaging back and forth with Christina the rest of the day and into the evening. She was circling around a single family that seemed to match up to a lot of my information.

The next morning I had a meeting for a charity committee I served on, and I let Christina know that I would be unavailable until lunchtime.

When I finished my meeting, I reached into my bag as I was walking across the quiet parking lot. It was a hot day, and the sun was bright. I found my sunglasses and put them on and immediately went back into my bag to search for my phone. I couldn't see the screen because the sun was too bright, so I walked to my car so I could check my messages.

I shut the door and rolled down the windows. It was sticky from the heat and humidity of the August air. I pulled my sunglasses up on top of my head and looked again at my phone. I had several notifications—missed calls, text messages, and emails. Some were messages from Christina. The first thing she had sent me was a photo. The photo was of my presumed biological maternal grandmother.

It was a black-and-white photograph, but I could tell from the photo that she had dark hair and dark eyes. The photo was a bit grainy, perhaps from a newspaper. Judging from the quality, it appeared old. Christina said she found out that the woman was a nurse, which was a match for the stories my mom had told me. Unfortunately, this woman had passed away in 1996. If she was my biological grandmother, and Christina *was* right, this would have been the woman who'd written the letter. She would be the person who'd sparked my interest in searching almost seven years ago, when I was twenty-six. I sat back in the hot leather seat and processed. I wondered if I would ever find out what was in that letter or if anyone else knew it existed. I messaged Christina back and thanked her for the photo and asked if she had any other information.

She did.

Christina had tracked down a photo of the woman's tombstone and her obituary. I watched as the three little dots of a response started and stopped over and over, anticipating the message. The first thing she sent was a link to the obituary, immediately followed by a lengthy paragraph.

She had two names in addition to my presumed biological maternal grandmother's name—the names of the woman's two daughters, Karen and Lynda.

*Lynda.*

As in the first three initials in the username? I asked Christina, "Could this be the same person in the user ID we were searching for before? LMW?"

"Yes, I think it is," she said.

*That means . . .*

That meant that Lynda was my DNA match. LMW was Lynda. Given her age and the degree of match, she would be my aunt. And if Lynda was my aunt, her sister Karen would be . . .

My birth mother.

Karen Jacobsen.

My birth mother was Karen Jacobsen.

A tidal wave of emotions hit me: relief, love, release, and wholeness. I burst into tears. They were dropping down my cheeks in the still-hot car faster than I could wipe them away. I stared at my phone in disbelief, holding it with my left hand, wiping tears with my right. I pulled the phone tight to my chest and let the tears fall.

I finally knew who they were.

Both of them.

I knew their names. I knew where they were from. I

knew some of their stories. I knew where they went to high school. I knew my grandparents' names. They were real. Real people with real stories and real names. Not just people I imagined, but real, tangible people.

Finally, after thirty-three years, I knew who my birth parents were.

I set my phone down on the warm dash and wiped my eyes with both hands. I sat up in the seat and buckled my seat belt. This was all so surreal. A part of me felt more complete than I ever had. Not only did I have the fullness of my gospel identity at my core, but now I had the missing link of my earthly history defined and named. God had answered my prayers. When I finally put Him first, He laid out the path to find them easily and quickly. It had only been five weeks since my trip to Ohio, and here we were. DNA matched, names, and real birth parents confirmed.

## Planned For

You know the feeling you have the eve of something big that's planned? Perhaps the night before you leave for a vacation or the night before a birthday party or a special occasion? That thrill and excitement that stirs inside of you, anxiously awaiting all the good that's about to unfold?

I wonder if that's how God feels when good things are about to happen to us, His kids. I wonder if that day, that hot summer day in August, if that was how God felt about me, about Karen, about Jim? Have you ever felt like something came together at just the right time? Or had that feeling that something great was about to happen? Much like Paul wrote to the Ephesians in Ephesians 1, God has plans for us:

> In him we have redemption through his
> blood, the forgiveness of our trespasses, accord-
> ing to the riches of his grace, which he lavished
> upon us, in all wisdom and insight, making
> known to us the mystery of his will, according
> to his purpose, which he set forth in Christ as a
> plan for the fullness of time, to unite all things
> in him, things in heaven and things on earth.
> (Ephesians 1:7–10)

There is such richness in these words. Not only does God promise redemption through grace, but Paul further explains how abundant God's plans are for us. In verse 8, Paul wrote, "which he lavished upon us." *Lavished.* The *Oxford Dictionary* defines *lavished* as "bestow something in generous or extravagant quantities on." I felt in this moment, as this plan, His plan, was unfolding, that He did indeed have an extravagant plan—not just for me but for us.

Further, as Paul explained in verse 9, "making known to us the mystery of his will." What was His will? Was He answering prayers, or could there be more? A bigger purpose? I didn't know yet what that will was, but I wondered if this experience of finding my birth parents was more than I realized or could comprehend. I suspected that this wasn't the end of the journey. There had to be more here than just me learning who my birth parents were. As I sat in my car that day, a little stirring in my heart felt like this wasn't it. There was more planned—I could feel it. As this passage of Scripture finishes in verse 10, "to unite all things in him, things in heaven and things on earth."

What if God planned this, all of this, in advance because He had something bigger planned—not just for me but for all of us? What if God's plans were bigger than I could see and bigger than I could have hoped for? What if God created *all* of us for such a time as this? After all, God is in the business of putting things back together. That's true for our hearts, our souls, and our circumstances.

I don't know how long I sat in that parking lot. It could have been five minutes, or it could have been an hour or more. I sat in my emotions, with tears still dripping off my chin. I needed to get back to work, although I didn't expect to get a whole lot done that afternoon.

I drove the short distance to my office and parked in the ramp. While I was walking to the office, I started googling both Lynda's and Karen's names. A ton of hits came up for Karen, but nothing in the Des Moines area. As I badged through the turnstile and walked toward the elevator, it occurred to me that perhaps one or both of them had been married and could have a different last name now. I started texting with my husband and asked if he had any ideas where I could find that information.

He suggested I look at Iowa Courts Online. If they had so much as had a speeding ticket, I might be able to find them there. If they had been divorced, that could show a name change also. In between meetings and emails, I kept searching. No luck. We were having some family friends over for dinner that night, so I had to pause my search and hustle home.

On my drive, I wondered, *Is it possible that I would come this far and not be able to get in touch with her?* What if I couldn't track her down? I started doubting. Most of all, I was scared this step would be just another dead end.

Another way of God showing me that this wasn't what defined me as a person. God designed me on purpose for a purpose, and getting in touch with my biological parents wasn't going to change that.

Or would it?

After dinner and conversation, I tucked my kids in. I had a couple work emails to send out to catch up from being out in the morning volunteering. By the time I finished up, I was exhausted. I checked in on the message I had sent to Jim to see if he had read it before calling it a night. He still had not read the message. Because we weren't connected, the message could sit in his "other" folder and be unseen for who knows how long.

## Messages

The next day, August 9, came and went—I was packed full of key meetings at work and didn't have a moment to spare. By the time my meetings ended at 5:00 p.m., I spent a few minutes reconnecting with Christina. She had found Lynda and Karen on Facebook and had sent me the links to their profiles. For some reason I couldn't send Karen a message. Her security must have been set to prevent it, but Lynda's was not. I looked at her profile carefully. This woman had long dark-brown hair, brown eyes, and a big smile. She went to the same high school that I knew my birth mother attended but was a few years behind her. Her first name was the first initial of the username I'd found, and her former last name matched the last initial in the user name. I felt confident Christina had found the right person. Everything checked out.

I took a deep breath. I prayed God would open her heart and that she would respond. I asked the Lord to nudge her to look in her messages and to see my note to her. I slowly typed and then sent her the following message:

> Lynda—I sent you a message on Ancestry. Hoping to ask you a couple questions about our DNA match. It appears we are a "close relative," which would be an aunt, grandma (you're far too young!!!), or half sibling.

I remembered to keep the message generic enough not to scare her away. I wanted to engage with her in hopes she would be willing to speak with me. I really didn't know what to expect, if anything, or how long I might be waiting before she would respond. I had read stories of people waiting years for responses, and I didn't want to get my hopes up.

But right here, in less than a week from getting my DNA matches back, I had figured out who both my birth parents were, tracked them down, and mustered up the courage to reach out to my DNA matches. I had played my full hand of moves. There was nothing left for me to do but wait.

The rest was up to God.

## Reflection

*Questions*
1. How would you describe God as the perfect Father?
2. What are some barriers for accepting God as the perfect parent?

3. What past hurts do you need to ask for God to carry for you? What would it look like to leave the pain of the past with God?

*Affirmations*
1. I do not need to carry the weight of my past.
2. I am worthy of God's forgiveness.
3. I am forgiven.

# *chapter nine*

## ACCEPTANCE

*For you formed my inward parts, you knitted me
together in my mother's womb. I praise you, for I
am fearfully and wonderfully made. Wonderful
are your works; my soul knows it very well. My
frame was not hidden from you, when I was
being made in secret, intricately woven in the
depths of the earth.*
Psalm 139:13–15

THE NEXT DAY WAS THURSDAY, AND it felt like the
longest week ever. Not only was I catching up from
being out of the office the week before, but I was really
struggling to focus. My team had been newly reorganized
under another leader, and I was spending time getting my
new manager up to speed on all the work my team was
doing.

I had just hit Send on an email containing a report I
owed her. I was on pins and needles awaiting any response

to the messages I had sent over the last few days. I had sent out messages to a total of four people: my paternal grandfather, my birth father, my paternal grandfather's sister, and my maternal aunt. How long would I wait for responses? Hours? No. Days? Weeks? Years? I had no idea what to expect, but I knew one thing for certain. God did not make me a patient person.

I sighed and sat back in my chair, glad to have the last item on my to-do list sent off for the day. I started to tidy up my office and pack up for the night when my phone vibrated. I reached for my phone and tipped the screen up just enough to see the call was from a 1-800 number I did not recognize. I hesitated in answering it. I pressed the side button to silence the ringer and went back to picking up my desk. It was after hours, and the office had emptied for the night. I was one of the last people there.

As I put away the last of the files, I glanced at my phone. The screen was lit up from a notification. I reached across my desk and picked up my phone with my left hand and almost dropped it from sheer shock.

I had a response.

I quickly typed in my password to unlock my phone. Scrolling quickly to my Facebook app, I navigated to the messages. My hands were shaking. I let out a forced breath. I closed my eyes and breathed in again as I opened the message. The response was to the Facebook message I had sent to the woman I believed to be my aunt Lynda, the younger sister of my birth mother.

"Just because she was responding does not mean it will be good news," I muttered before looking back down. "It does not mean it will be the answer I have been hoping for. It might not be good." I was preparing myself for the worst.

I opened the message. I reread what I had sent her the day before:

Lynda—I sent you a message on Ancestry. Hoping to ask you a couple questions about our DNA match. It appears we are a "close relative," which would be an aunt, grandma (you're far too young!!!), or half sibling.

Her response took my breath away. I truly felt like my heart stopped beating.

*Yes, I believe you are my sister's daughter. I am your aunt.*

I held the phone with both hands now, to steady it, almost like an open-handed prayer. I read the words over and over again. I could feel the thud-thud of my heart beating again in my throat. A single tear ran down my right cheek, dropping onto my lap. I felt as if all the blood had drained out of my head and was sitting in a big lump in my stomach. I read the words again: *Yes, I believe you are my sister's daughter. I am your aunt.*

I read it over and over again. My fingers started moving to respond. Deep down in my heart, I knew this was the answer. I knew she was my aunt. There was no other explanation. But to see it there, so clearly, so matter of fact, completed a piece of my puzzle, a piece of who I was and where I came from. And I felt relief.

"I think you are right . . . wow!" I responded.

*I can't believe it.* Just like that—in plain, simple text— real confirmation of what I had suspected was true for just less than twenty-four hours but had searched seven years to find. There it was, affirmation, acknowledgment, even . . . acceptance. A real confirmation of my birth mother, both who she was and that she was mine. I sat still, reading the words over and over again. I needed to call David, but I felt unsure what to say or where to start. I took a picture of myself with the biggest smile and tears on my cheeks and texted it to him. Next, I touched the Phone icon on my Home screen, pressed Favorites and the first number, "Hubs." I sent the picture and then quickly answered his immediate call.

"What's going on? Are you okay?" he asked, skipping hello.

"She responded—Lynda—she responded. She said she thinks . . . she thinks . . . that, um, that I'm her sister's daughter . . . that she's my aunt. She really responded. It is her. Karen is my birth mother."

I could barely get the words out.

Right then my phone vibrated as I received another message on Messenger. Messenger asked if I wanted to accept a message from a person I didn't know. Normally I would think twice and then reject that prompt. But given the circumstances, I accepted the message.

It was her. Karen Jacobsen. The woman who I believed was my birth mother. The name I had only known for less than one day. She was real—and alive—and reaching out to me.

She had sent me a wave!

I immediately responded with *Hi!!!* which was all I could think to say.

She responded immediately.

"David, hang on a second. I just got a message from my birth mother. Just hang on a second; let me read it."

Her message was so simple and let me know right away that she was not going to reject me. It simply read, *I love you.*

The tears fell again, this time with velocity. Not a few one by one, but big tears. All the doubt, the worry she might not want anything to do with me, not want to contact me, not want to know who I was, or to simply not want to open that chapter of her life, all washed away. A sense of relief cascaded over me. All the weight of my past, the fear of rejection and worry of what might happen, lifted.

The tears started dripping onto my hands and the screen of my phone before I could begin to wipe them away. I rested my forearms on my thighs and rested my forehead in my right hand. I closed my eyes and let the tears drop. It was all I could do to not sob in my office, but I could not stop the tears from falling. My nose had started to run, and I was sniffling.

I lifted my head up to navigate to a tissue and wiped my nose. I was so thankful the office had emptied and I could sit in this moment. It was surreal. Time seemed to slow as I looked back at my phone and tried to find the words to say back. I stared at the screen for what felt like a long time. After a few moments I finally typed out a short message. *I can't believe this! After 33 years, I never thought I would find you.* More tears fell. I was holding my breath, just about the time three little dots appeared on the screen.

*Ditto. Do you have time to meet?*

Suddenly I snapped back to reality out of the haze of the moment, and I gasped.

Loudly.

Poor David was still waiting on the other end of the phone, awaiting the details of what was happening. For a moment I had forgotten he was still on the line.

"David, she wants to meet me. Like now. Do you think that I could go do that? Go meet her? I mean, well, should I go meet her? I don't know her, I guess?"

He laughed loudly, like this was the craziest question I had ever asked—and perhaps it was. "Yes." He chuckled. "Of course you can go meet her—we've got everything under control here. You go meet your birth mom."

My vision blurred with tears again, and I pursed my lips and nodded. This was happening.

"Okay," I said confidently. "I'm going to . . . I am going to meet my birth mom! Wow. Okay. I'll, um, I'll see you later then, I guess! Love you. And hey, babe. Thanks."

"Of course. Have fun!"

And with that, I hung up. Stunned, I sat there for a moment. Holy crap. I was going to go meet my birth mom. I looked around my desk side to side, doing a quick check to see if there was anything I needed to do. I quickly shoved my laptop into my bag and locked my file cabinet. I felt my phone vibrate again. This time it was from a man named Kyle. Same last name as Karen. Who could this be?

I accepted the message from Kyle as I stood up and walked out of my office, turning off the light switch. The message simply read: *Hey, I'm your brother. I'll let you chat with Karen.*

My jaw dropped, and I stopped suddenly.

*A brother.*

Of course, I had always thought I might have siblings—but they hadn't been the primary focus of my search. All these years I had thought even if I found my biological parents, they might not want to meet me, for starters, but also, they might not want to incorporate or even mention me to their families. I had read so many stories of rejection. Stories where birth parents (especially teen parents) wanted to keep their mistake—their child—hidden forever. But here I was, exchanging messages with this man who said he was my brother. I started walking again, toward the elevator bank. I pressed the Down button.

*I'm blown away*, I typed. *I've been praying for this day for my whole life!*

*So am I. This is crazy.*

*I can't wait to get to know you*, I responded, with a smiley face. *Do you live in Des Moines too?* The elevator dinged, and I stepped inside, pressing the button for the lobby. The doors shut and the elevator started to go down.

"Yes, I am currently living with mom," he said.

Holy cow . . . I wonder how old he is. I suspected that I could have siblings, but I kinda assumed if I did they would be early twenties by now, given my birth parents' ages at the time of my birth. I wondered if he was younger than I'd expected, given he was still living with Karen. *Hmm . . . I better ask.* The doors opened, and I stepped into the lobby, still glued to my phone, waiting for texts. I headed toward the parking ramp while I exchanged messages with my newfound brother.

*May I ask how old you are?*

*I'll be 30 in November—there's four years between us.*

*Oh wow! How awesome!*
*This is so crazy.*
*Um, yeah! Words can't really describe it! Was just a regular work day until about 30 minutes ago.*
*I'm still blown away.*

I realized I had taken the parking ramp elevator to the wrong floor because my car was nowhere to be found. I marched up the ramp to the next level to find it. Still no car. I was so engrossed, I had managed to get lost in the parking ramp.

After a few more texts to Karen and Kyle, Karen and I decided to meet at a coffee shop just ten minutes from my office. Once I finally managed to find my car and slide inside, I blotted the last of the tears from my face. I looked down at what I was wearing—all white, with a beige open sweater. I normally would have stressed about what to wear, what I looked like, but in this moment, I realized that it didn't matter. Even though the underlying fear of rejection was still with me, I knew I could go through this because I had the safety and security of the Father with me. He had accepted me no matter what happened next. I was comforted and calm. God was with me.

I drove the short distance to the coffee shop. I navigated the tight parking lot outside and found one of the last remaining spots. My heart was pounding so loudly, I could barely think. I slid out of my car and walked across the parking lot to enter in the side door. The shop was packed. The indoor area was full of fifties-diner décor and was mostly arranged in small booths and tables. There was not an open table in sight. Expecting this to be an emotional meeting, I scanned for a discreet place to sit. Not seeing anything indoors, I spotted a little table outside, tucked away from the others.

Perfect.

## Waiting

As I sat waiting, I reflected back on the journey to get to this place. So much had happened since I first learned about the letter. At that time, I was twenty-six, newly pregnant, and processing the fact that somewhere out there was a message my maternal grandmother had wanted me to read one day. Since that moment, I had grown in my faith. What started as a search for who I was turned into the full knowledge of who God said I was. The script had been flipped. No longer had I desired to meet my birth parents to feel complete, but I desired to know them to know who they were.

It had been only a mere few weeks since I'd prayed from that new perspective, and God clearly outlined, step by step, exactly what to do and placed specific people in my path at specific times to track down just the right details and the right clues to lead me to this very moment. I was minutes away from meeting the person who brought me into this world. In this moment, it was abundantly clear to me. *Our faith does not change God's promises. God's promises change our faith.* His promise of love, acceptance, and redemption was playing out in real time right before my eyes. As Jesus said in Matthew 6:10, "Your will be done, on earth as it is in heaven."

This sure felt like heaven to me. God's will be done.

There was no other way this moment would be happening without God's will. That I was very sure of.

## Reflection

### Questions

1. How would you describe true acceptance?
2. Who in your life makes you feel that way?
3. How is that different from how others make you feel?

### Affirmations

1. God accepts me for who I am.
2. I do not need to earn acceptance from God.
3. I accept myself for who I am.

*chapter ten*

## MEETING HER

*You formed me with your hands; you made me.*
Job 10:8 NLT

THE SUN WAS STARTING TO DIP down over the bridge
in the distance. The coffee shop was situated near a
major on-ramp to the interstate, and the rush-hour traffic
was heavy. Cars passed on the nearby street close to where
I was waiting. The buzz of the traffic served as a good dis-
traction while I waited for Karen. I sent David a quick text
message to let him know where we had decided to meet
and that I was guessing it would be a few hours before I was
home. He was encouraging, wishing me luck, and told me
not to worry. He had everything covered with the kids, so
I could stay as long as I wanted.

I sent Karen a message, letting her know I had found
a table and was outside facing the street. I explained that
I was tall, like her, five feet ten inches, and also had dark

hair. I thought about how strange it was to know all these things about someone but not actually know them. This was all about to change. Karen messaged me back to let me know she was on her way and wasn't too far from the coffee shop. What was separated for thirty-three years was about to be restored.

I had my back to the interior of the coffee shop and was looking out at the road. This felt like an out-of-body experience. An hour ago I was having a regular day, and now I was waiting to meet my birth mother for the first time. I still couldn't believe it. I think I was in shock.

I moved my work bag from my lap into the extra chair, assuming I would stand when she arrived. Would we hug? While I was still pondering over what it would be like in our first few moments meeting, I saw a woman, about five foot ten, with long brown hair and a big smile, walking right toward me. She was beaming ear to ear. I smiled ear to ear back.

"Hi!" She walked right up to me and opened up her arms. I stood up quickly. With heels on, I was slightly taller, but I could tell we were almost the same height.

"Hi, wow!" I said back, embracing her for the first time.

We hugged for a long time, soaking in the moment. This was her, the woman who brought me into this world, my birth mom. She gave me away so I could have better—a better life. She gave my mom a child and the family she always desired to have. It was because of Karen's choice that all of that happened.

I felt immense gratitude toward her. As I held her in my arms, I felt so thankful for her and so thankful that

God had brought us together. As we released from our first hug and sat down, I thought about all the things I wanted to say to her. For as long as I had been alive, I wondered about her. Before I had the desire to meet her, before I'd learned about the letter, I'd fantasized about what she was like. I could tell right away that she had a caring, loving heart.

We started to pull apart and held hands, as if to freeze this moment in our minds. This wasn't a moment either of us would forget. As we sat down, we both wiped tears that had graced our respective faces.

Karen was the first to speak. "What took you so long?" We both let out a bit of a laugh. She wiped tears off one cheek and then the next.

I smiled. "Well, you were sort of difficult to find!"

She asked me how long I had been searching, and I explained that I had just learned about the letter when I turned twenty-six, seven years ago, when I was pregnant with our first child, and that learning about the letter was what sparked my interest to search. I told her I was always curious but hadn't really considered searching until I had learned about it. She asked me how long I had known I was adopted, and I told her I always knew. I shared that my dad was also adopted and had wanted me to know that from the start. Karen shared that she had been told that, and it was a major factor in her choosing my parents. I told her about looking on and off all these years and that it was only just a few weeks ago that I had learned about Ancestry's DNA test and had submitted a form to register with the International Soundex Reunion Registry at the same time.

I explained how I had worked with a genealogical search angel to help figure out who Lynda was and to send her a message on Facebook, only the day before. Even though the search took years, the process had unfolded so quickly. It was as if the path was clearly illuminated in front of me and all I had to do was trust the nudges God presented and to keep taking each step forward. I told her I had read stories of people who would search for their birth parents their entire lives only to be rejected and that I was fairly overwhelmed with how this unfolded. I told her I was shocked that I'd searched periodically for the last seven years, and yet all of a sudden, I was able to find her so easily.

Karen explained that she too had been searching for me for many years. I was shocked to hear this. I had been told that she had chosen to surrender me for adoption because she wanted to give me a better life. What I learned that night turned what I knew about my adoption upside down. It was a lot to digest.

## Creation

I was a product of teen pregnancy. That was clear. Karen was sixteen when I was conceived and born, and yes, she confirmed my birth father to be Jim. There was no escaping the fact that my creation was because of a sinful act. Throughout my life I struggled with being the product of a sin. As I grew in my faith, I struggled with this even more. Because my origin was as result of premarital sex, I had been labeled and called terrible things as a child. Everything from being called unwanted to being called a bastard child. I carried this around for a long time. What had changed in the months prior to this moment was the understanding that what other people thought about my origin wasn't what mattered. Further, despite the fact that my birth parents sinned, which resulted in my creation, that did not mean that I wasn't chosen by God. That I did not have purpose.

I learned that God used our circumstances to bring glory to Him. The Bible is very clear that we are all created by God. There is not a qualifier to that statement. Isaiah 64:8 states, "And yet, O Lord, you are our Father. We are the clay, and you are the potter. We are all formed by your hand." I have searched the Scriptures and have not once found anything that suggests a qualifier for that statement. Not once does God say a baby isn't part of His plan. In fact, we have seen God use a baby to drive unity among people before. A baby was God's plan to save the world, after all. He did send us baby Jesus.

## Rebellion

Karen shared about her pregnancy. She'd been forced to change schools and was treated horribly by her parents and her peers. She was called the worst names you can imagine. She refused to have the abortion her parents urged her to have. Because of her age, being a minor, she was forced to put me up for adoption by her parents. It was not her choice, and it broke her heart. Sitting with her that night, I not only heard these words, but I could feel it too. Learning this broke my heart too. I had always been told that she wanted to put me up for adoption, that it was her choice to do that to give me a better life. But what I learned that cool summer evening was more about the untold darker side of adoption. The side of adoption that often isn't discussed. Adoptees have no choice to be adopted; we just are. It shapes our identities whether we want it to or not. It is a part of us. It is challenging at times. However, for birth parents, what I learned was, it can be far worse.

It was heartrending to hear from Karen about how she was treated while she was pregnant and as a part of my adoption. The thing most people don't want to hear or acknowledge is that adoption isn't always beautiful or a blessing for everyone involved. In this case, because Karen was a minor, the decision to choose adoption hadn't landed with her. What I learned from her in this reunion moment I will never forget. Hearing for the very first time that my birth mother did not want to give me up and in fact was forced to, pained me to my core.

Can you imagine being an adoptive parent and knowing the child you are adopting, while completing your desire for a family, was ripping another apart? No, of course not. That's why it's not shared. My parents were not told this part of the story. They were told a different story. That Karen wanted to give me a better life. That she was happy about the decision. What I learned this day was that both parents were lied to. The information was fabricated by the attorneys to close the transaction.

I also learned that Karen was told some things about my parents that weren't necessarily true. My parents' financial status was exaggerated to make them look better in the eyes of Karen and her parents. My parents were told that it was my biological maternal grandmother who'd wanted to keep me but that Karen wanted to provide a different life for me. When in fact the opposite was true. My maternal grandmother forced Karen to put me up for adoption.

As heartbreaking as this was to hear, it also brought some healing.

What I learned that day was I was desired all along. Karen always wanted me, and that healed a wound of rejection I had pushed deep inside since my childhood. Being able to fully heal that wound would take time, but I now knew it to be possible. That wound healed as I learned that God had chosen me and I was never rejected or forsaken by Him. There was a small part of me that still saw value in the acceptance of the people I loved. This was an issue I needed to work through, as I was still seeking some level of acceptance and approval from people. I was still holding on to that societal acceptance, when I needed to be fully focused on the acceptance that I did not need to earn—the acceptance of the Lord.

Karen and I continued to discuss our stories throughout the evening. I told her a couple of things that were really important for me to say to her. I told her that what she did by signing the papers to release me to my adoptive parents did give me a fantastic life. I told her I'd been raised as an only child but had been involved in sports and activities. I'd gone to college and gotten a master's degree in accounting. I told her I was married and had two kids, which meant she had grandkids. I told her I was loved and that I hoped she could feel peace knowing I was well taken care of. I also told her I didn't want to put pressure on her for anything she wasn't comfortable with. I didn't know what her expectations were in regard to our relationship, but I definitely was hoping she would be willing to share more information with me about her family.

## Timing

She said she'd registered with the International Search Soundex around the time I turned eighteen. Of course, that had been many years ago, long before DNA testing was a widely available option and certainly before I had decided I wanted to search for my birth parents. Although it must have been painful for Karen to wait, I think back about what was happening in our lives at the time when she had been searching, and I know that if she had tracked me down at that time, I would not have been ready. My father had been very ill, dying from cancer, and my heart would not have been open to or available for such a reunion. I smiled and looked down, because I knew that must be hard to hear. But I could see how God's hands wrapped around our reunion, to protect us both from possible rejection, which certainly would have ruined a chance of the reconciliation we both clearly desired.

Karen was very clear she was very willing to share anything I could possibly want to know about her or her family and that it was her desire without question to have a relationship with me and my family if we would have her. I could see in our exchange over the short few hours that this reunion meant more to her than I would ever understand.

Over the next three hours, we shared a lot of stories. I learned so much about her, my brother Kyle, how she grew up, and what the last thirty-three years had held for her. It was interesting to learn about the adoption process from her side. Learning that she had not wanted to put me up for adoption was easily the most shocking news she shared with me, but it made sense that the attorney would lie about that. It made the adoption story for the adoptive parents easier. I had read numerous stories about this same situation online. I just didn't think it would be our story too.

There was so much more I wanted to learn. I wanted to get to know her better, to learn about my origin, and about our family. We agreed to meet again later in the week and exchanged phone numbers. I offered to bring photos the next time we met.

We stood up and hugged again.

I would never forget this moment.

After we pushed in our chairs, we walked through the patio and toward the parking lot.

"Would you like me to walk you to your car?" I felt a responsibility to ensure she was safe. The neighborhood could be a bit dangerous, and it was well past dark by now.

"Oh no, I'm okay."

"All right, well, good night," I said as we embraced again under the dim streetlight.

"Good night, sweetie. Be safe," Karen said as we parted ways.

I pressed the Unlock button on my key fob and climbed into my car.

I felt euphoric. A million things ran through my mind—none of which had anything to do with driving home. I turned on my car and sat there for several minutes in awe. In awe of God's timing. On the micro level, He waited until I hit Send on that report, which had been the crucible of my week. On a macro level, I didn't know why now—why not some other time in my life. Why not sooner? Why not years ago? There was this shred of disappointment that I would never know my biological maternal grandmother—never know what she wanted me to know in that letter.

But it didn't matter. I had met her—Karen—my birth mother, the woman who chose life, who chose me. The joy of meeting her, and getting to thank her for what she did by surrendering me for adoption, was an answered prayer I would never, ever forget.

I teared up again, and as the tears dropped, I put my car in drive and headed home, thanking God for this day.

A day I will never, ever forget.

## Reflection

*Questions*

1. How might God be using you to bless other people already?
2. What are ways you could bless others today, this week, or this month?
3. Describe two to three times when God used you to help others.

*Affirmations*

1. God will use me to bless others.
2. I am confident the work God has planned for me is good.
3. The plans the Lord has for me will be completed.

# chapter eleven

## ABUNDANCE

*O Lord, I will honor and praise your name,*
*for you are my God.*
*You do such wonderful things!*
*You planned them long ago,*
*and now you have accomplished them.*

Isaiah 25:1 CSB

BY AUGUST 15 I STILL HADN'T heard back from Jim. A few days earlier I'd seen that he'd finally read the message, but no response. While I was disappointed, a part of me wasn't too surprised. I would reach out to him again to try to get any relevant medical information, then I would let it go. Since he had read my message but hadn't responded, I assumed that what I knew about him was true—he hadn't been involved then and likely didn't want to be involved now.

I wasn't ready to disappear without the information

I desired. I had found my birth mother and birth father. That alone had answered so many of my prayers.

Karen clearly wanted to be involved in my life, which was beyond my wildest imagination. I spent the evening with her at the library. We shared old photos and stories about our lives. I had brought pictures of myself as a little girl, my wedding album, and photos of my kids. I also brought two things my mother had given me the day she'd given me the letter: a stuffed Christmas doll from the hospital gift shop and a bib that read *I'm a Lutheran baby*, referring to the hospital where I was born.

Karen brought similar items: old photos, a CD of family pictures, and letters she had written me over the years, to my name at birth, Amanda. It was so strange to think of myself with another name, yet many adoptees do have other names prior to their adoptions. In Iowa that information is sealed in state records that we cannot gain access to.

When home from the library, I warmed up leftovers and decided I was done waiting for Jim to respond. I didn't need anything from him other than some medical information. I wrote a second message to Jim. This time, I took a more matter-of-fact approach, as I had nothing to lose. I didn't need a relationship with him—I simply wanted some answers.

> Hi Jim. It's been about a week and a half since I sent you the last message, and I've been able to piece enough together to know that you are my biological father. I have two children of my own, and I would really like to get in touch with you, at the very least to understand medi-

cal risks I may be passing on to them from your side. Thanks again, Wendy

## Finally

The next day was packed with meetings and flew by. I raced home from work to relieve our neighbor girl, who was watching the kids for the day, and helped David put the final touches on dinner. Later, after we tucked the kids in and I was preparing to start my homework for my MBA program, my phone dinged.

> Wendy,
> First off, wow. Clearly this comes as a bit of a surprise to say the least. Brings up a wide range of emotions and questions.

We exchanged a few messages throughout the evening, starting with me explaining how I'd determined we were related through the DNA match, given he had not taken a DNA test. While there was a plethora of information, I simply stuck to the DNA, as that was the most concrete evidence and the easiest to explain. I shared that because of the DNA match to his father, I knew, since he was his father's only son, he was my birth father. I shared a screen shot of the match I had to his father from Ancestry.com to provide evidence of the match.

Without getting into any of the other evidence that pointed to him, I carefully and delicately explained that there were a couple of things I wanted to say right away, hoping to not scare him away. He was responding to my messages and participating in our exchange. However, I didn't know if or for how long he might continue. I wanted to get a couple of things out to put him at ease. I explained that I shared the same things with Karen the night we met.

> The choice you made, to put me up for adoption, gave me a great life. My parents were loving; I had access to any opportunity I wanted. I was raised as an only child—I went to college, earned an undergraduate degree in accounting and an MIS, have a graduate degree in accounting, taught classes at Drake, am happily married, and I have two children. I'm happy. Everything is ok over here. ☺

I carefully continued our conversation, explaining that I had nothing but respect for him and Karen, for making the impossible choice to put me up for adoption. As a parent myself, I couldn't imagine making that decision.

## Our Past, Our History

Looking back over the years of our lives, we are faced with times that were not exactly what one had hoped for. This exchange had to bring back memories for Jim. But regardless of what happened to Jim, or what happens to us, our past is part of our story. Whether we have chosen to hide part of our life or be open, it is still a part of us. I assured Jim I had carefully reached out to him so as to not "out" him or our situation, because he might not have told a soul that I existed and might never want to. We all have secrets, and I was astutely aware that I might be one.

I did caution that because I matched to his dad on Ancestry, there was a risk his father would see our match and my generic message to him eventually. He might never see it; he might see it and not care. He might already know I existed and not want anything to do with me. All of those options were in front of me. I was aware that I could very well be on the verge of rejection.

Then this really amazing thing happened.

Instead of getting nervous or disappearing . . .

Jim asked me questions. *About me.* About when I started searching, why I started searching, and what I had found. I explained that I had always known I was adopted, that my parents were always open and honest with me about that, and it was a part of who I was. We quickly figured out that we had a lot in common. We both had worked in public accounting right out of college. We had lived near each other for over a decade in two separate parts of the city. I slowly walked him through the details of my search, the whole process.

Our conversation went on late into the night, and I also asked him questions. I learned that his family didn't know about me. Since he was eighteen when I was born (although seventeen at the time I was conceived), he hadn't told a soul. He asked me when I had found Karen. He was as shocked as I was to learn how fast this had all come together. We uncovered we knew some of the same people, which was wild. Given we lived in the same town our whole lives, we'd likely crossed paths many times over my life and had no idea. We quickly uncovered that we even attended the same church, Lutheran Church of Hope!

I felt such a peace after our first exchange. Even though

it was over Facebook Messenger, I was so thankful that he was open to exchanging messages with me, engaged in our conversation, curious about me, and seemed open to further discussion. I went to bed more at ease than I had been in the month and a half since I'd started down this road. I had found them both. Neither of them had rejected me. I'd found them.

I'd found my birth family.

God lined up all the stars, prepared all our hearts, and here we were. All three of us.

## Now What

The next day Jim sent me the first message. I was relieved to see it pop up. I didn't want to push too hard, but I had so many more questions. I did want to ask him about medical risks still, though he seemed a bit more curious about me than I ever would have guessed. I trusted we would get there eventually. He genuinely seemed like a nice man who wanted to learn more about me. He kindly asked if he could ask me questions, and of course I obliged. He was curious what his father might see on Ancestry or what the chances were that he might already have found that I had matched to him. I offered to show him everything, and I did. I walked him through the exact paperwork I had and how it lined up with the records I'd searched, and I even shared my spreadsheet with him with screen shots of all the records embedded. I suppose there are benefits to having an auditing background—great documentation and data analysis.

We went back and forth most of the day. Eventually we

did get into medical information. He shared openly and candidly what he knew.

But we kept exchanging messages. It was all positive, and I felt a bond forming.

He gently asked if I would be willing to take a paternity test, to further confirm the data and research. He assured me he was 99 percent sure I was right, but he wanted to remove any doubt.

I had no concerns or hesitations about affirming what I already knew to be true. If this additional step could bring him peace, I was more than happy to do it.

I had what I had come for, but I smiled. It had started out as a small smirk but quickly spread across my face to an ear-to-ear smile. The fact that he wanted to confirm this information meant one thing—because, frankly, I had what I needed.

There was definitely more here.

I didn't know what it was or what might happen, but this man was engaging in conversation, wanting to know more about me, and wanting absolute assurance that I was his.

I needed to keep going to see what might come of this.

## Testing

Over the next few days, we continued to get to know each other. It was clear we had a similar sense of humor. We joked about the oddity of taking a paternity test at our respective ages. I was thirty-three and married, yet here I was googling *How to take a paternity test*. I had no idea how this worked, but now I was trying to figure out how to complete one. After about an hour of searching, I found one that could be purchased online, completed at home via a quick mouth swab and mailed in. Results were promised quickly, for an upgrade fee, of course.

Jim and I decided that in the unlikely chance that the result wasn't a match, we didn't want to meet, at least not with the information lingering. I continued to stay silent about meeting. I wasn't confident that was what he wanted, and I didn't want to ask or push.

We planned a way to pass the test back and forth without meeting. Given we had both done a fair amount of checking into the other person, both out of curiosity and safety, we knew where each other lived. Jim purchased the kit, and on Saturday, August 15, he left it on my front porch while we were away for the morning. I took my portion of the test and drove it back to Jim's house while he was away so he could mail it in.

It felt like forever between that Saturday and the day we got our results.

Throughout the waiting process, Jim continued to pour into our new relationship. Despite the pending results, we texted back and forth daily. I confirmed I had no expectations, yet he shared he planned to tell his family, including his kids, about me.

That blew me away. I never expected to be accepted this openly by my birth parents, for just being me. I did nothing to earn their love, but yet here we were. God had prepared their hearts for this reunion in advance, and with each passing moment, I was in awe of what He had done. He had never failed me. Even in the darkest of times, God had held true to His word for us. While the Enemy intends bad things to hurt us, God uses everything for good. Although a teen pregnancy was not exactly planned, God knew this would happen, and He used thirty-three years to plan this beautiful reunion for the good of the three of us.

## Results

By Wednesday, August 23, results day, we were both on edge. Even though I was 100 percent confident in the results, I knew this confirmation would change things. I felt deeply that we were on the verge of solidifying where I would sit in Jim's life.

I decided to work from home. It was a beautiful sunny day, which was perfect, because it was my daughter's first day of first grade. She was beaming ear to ear all morning, excited to meet her new teacher and see her friends. I cleared my schedule that morning so we could take first-day photos at home, I could drive her to school, and I could walk her to her class. Although I was excited for her first day, I knew today was the day I'd find out the results of the paternity test. I knew what they were going to say—that wasn't why I was anxious.

I was anxious because Jim would get the confirmation he needed, to know without any doubt that he was my birth father. That finality would clear any barriers and leave me with just one question: What would the future hold if Jim knew I was for sure his biological daughter?

The day crept by. Each hour felt like five. I logged in at the top of every hour to check the results. Nothing. By the time two o'clock rolled around, I worried that the results wouldn't be ready. I don't know how we would make it another day. We were both anxious and full of emotion.

A few minutes after 2:00 p.m., my email chimed. I raced to log in, and there, in clear black and white, was the confirmation.

Jim was my birth father.

My eyes welled with tears. Despite feeling confident going into the test, I was overcome with emotion to see it in front of me.

I sent Jim a message, letting him know the results confirmed what we suspected.

He sent me back one word.

*Speechless.*

*Me too,* I responded. Time seemed to stand still. I had difficulty finding any words. I simply asked, *How do you feel now?*

*A bundle of emotions. None of them bad, just a mix of excitement, joy, and trying not to cry.*

The tears I had been choking back spilled over one by one and dropped into my lap.

His next message said he wanted to meet me. And soon.

## Reflection

*Questions*

1. How can you more closely walk with the Lord?
2. What could you do to deepen your relationship with the Lord today, this week, this month?
3. What might change as a result of a closer walk?

*Affirmations*

1. God wants to be in a relationship with me.
2. God desires to be close to me.
3. I can turn to God anywhere, anytime.

# *chapter twelve*

## REDEEMED

*None of the good promises the Lord*
*had made to the house of Israel failed.*
*Everything was fulfilled.*
Joshua 21:45 CSB

LATER THAT DAY JIM LET ME know he was planning to meet with his dad as soon as possible to tell him the news. I couldn't quite wrap my mind around what it would be like to sit down with your dad after over thirty years and tell him you have another child that you never told him about—but that was what Jim was preparing to do. His dad was preparing to leave the country on a trip for several weeks, and Jim wanted to catch him before he left.

I was still in a fog, finding it surreal that just earlier today we'd received results, and now he was off to meet with his dad to tell him about me.

Jim asked me to pray for him and his dad, which I was happy to do. He texted me right before he went in to meet him and then twenty minutes later.

Turns out Grandpa Jim was thrilled. He'd known Jim had signed the papers for my adoption for over thirty years (the question of how remains a bit unclear to this day). Jim told me that Grandpa Jim was joyful about hearing the news and became choked up. He teased Jim endlessly about being a grandpa now himself. He encouraged Jim to share the news with the rest of his family, which was overwhelming. This was quickly moving from *found my birth father* to *you now have this huge extended group of people who know about you.* I hadn't thought much beyond Jim and his two teenage kids. Suddenly that family tree was growing.

**Meeting Jim**

The next day, Thursday, Jim told me he was ready to meet me. He wanted to meet before telling anyone else, and he expressed some urgency, asking if I could meet as soon as the next day. I was in class all day for my MBA program but could make the evening work. His kids were headed to a football game, and he could meet me then without them getting suspicious. We aligned on a time and place—7:00 p.m. at Panera. He had met his dad there the night before and said it was quiet, empty, and discreet. We left it a bit tentative, in case his kids' plans changed.

**Blessings from Others**

I barely slept the that night. The next day was a blur. I tried to focus in class, but my mind was elsewhere. I had pulled together photos from my childhood that I had shared with Karen two weeks prior and was as ready as I was going to be to meet my birth father. I had no idea what to expect it to feel like to see him for the first time. We had exchanged so many messages that I had a good sense for his personality. But meeting someone face to face for the first time, well, that just different. I was nervous.

He had one more person to meet with before he met with me—his girlfriend of six years, Lynn. Now that he had DNA results and had told his dad, Lynn was the most important person for Jim to share this news with, before he shared it any further. He was planning to meet with her a few hours before our planned meetup. As expected, she was shocked, according to Jim. Who could blame her? We were all shocked. The speed at which this unfolded still baffled me. Even though I had searched for years before, it was as if God had been waiting for me to firmly place my identity in Him, and then He opened up the floodgates so I could find these people who had suddenly become so important to me, in an instant.

Jim said Lynn gave him a big hug when he told her, which reassured me. Since Jim seemed interested in getting to know me, I suspected the only reasons he wouldn't would be because of his kids' or his girlfriend's wishes. Her support mattered a great deal to me even though I didn't know her.

I arrived at Panera a few minutes early. My head was spinning, and my heart was racing. My hands were sweating and shaking, clasped together as if in prayer.

"I don't think I have ever been this nervous about anything in my whole life," I muttered under my breath while parking the car and turning off the ignition. I suppose there is no perfect place to meet your dad for the first time—but this sounded like a good enough option. The parking lot was nearly empty, and only a few people were inside.

I sent Jim a text to let him know I was there. He responded and said he was a few minutes away.

*I'm nervous as hell!* he said.

Well, that was good. It wasn't just me then. *Me too*, I responded. *I think my stomach is in my throat.* I texted David one last time to let him know I had made it to Panera before tucking my phone into my bag next to the photo albums of my kids, loose pictures of me as a baby, and the paperwork from my adoption. I pursed my lips and exhaled forcefully. It was time. I opened the car door.

It was nice out the kind of warm summer day where it's not too hot before sunset but still just cool enough that you wanted to be outside. The birds were chirping, and I thought for a moment about sitting outside. Looking at the patio, I saw that several tables were occupied by other people. I hesitated, thinking it might be uncomfortable if we were sitting right next to another table, given the conversation I anticipated us having and the tears I expected to shed.

As I entered the restaurant, I thought that never in a million years would I have expected to be walking into a Panera on a Friday night to meet a stranger who just happened to be my biological father. I still couldn't believe this was happening. I smiled. God was sure up to something.

I looked around for the quietest place. My eyes settled

on a booth near the entrance, and I slid into the seat with my back to the door. I didn't want to make eye contact with him when he walked in, for fear I would cry instantly. There was no way I was going to get through this without serious tears. I could feel my heart beating in my throat, pounding harder. I wrung my hands under the table, trying to calm my nerves. I tried to think of something to tell myself to lower my anxiety but kept coming up blank. What exactly do you tell yourself before meeting your dad for the first time? Most people are babies, after all, and probably aren't thinking much except *What the heck is this place? It's so bright here.* I managed to smirk at my silly thought.

I heard the door behind me open and shut. I drew in a labored breath as my heart raced.

Out of the corner of my eye, I saw a man, who looked equally as anxious as I felt, walk toward me, and we locked eyes. The corners of his mouth turned up slightly in a nervous smile.

"Hi," he said.

I nervously smiled back at him. "Hi," I replied as I slid out of the booth and stood to give him a hug. *Wow. This is really happening.* Everything seemed to stand still. I opened my arms and embraced him as he hugged me back.

This first moment seemed so surreal—the moment that I had thought about since I first saw his picture a few weeks ago, first contacted him, first exchanged messages with him. It was a feeling like I had never experienced. As I stood there hugging a man I had only just met, I realized what I was feeling. Love. And it felt so natural.

Love.

Instantly.

My jaw dropped as I continued to wrap my arms around him for what felt like hours and mere seconds at the same time. I was so surprised that I felt this way that I just kept hugging him, unable to move, shocked at the emotion and terrified it would stop. I opened my eyes briefly and noticed the restaurant was mostly empty except for another table several yards away and a few employees. One employee had been sweeping the floor but had seen us embracing and had stopped to stare at us. We must have been embracing a long time.

"People . . . people are staring at us," I managed to stammer. But neither of us cared. After a few more minutes—or was it seconds?—we sat in the booth, facing each other. Neither of us said a word for a long time.

I couldn't remember the last time I was speechless.

"Wow." Jim finally broke the silence.

I let out a breath I must have been holding. I was no longer nervous, just in awe of the moment, of the circumstances. *I can't believe this is happening. That I'm sitting here with my biological father.*

I realized we were both sitting with our left hand supporting our chins in the same way. I shifted my weight and moved slightly. It was just so weird to look at someone who looked a lot like you, for the first time. We had the same eyes, nose, and chin. My smile definitely came from Karen, but the lines around my mouth were definitely from Jim. None of this felt real.

Jim glanced down at his phone. His dad was texting him. Urging him to hurry up and tell his sister, my aunt, about me. Grandpa Jim and his wife, Sandy, had driven to stay with my new aunt before heading out of the country.

Then, a second text showed up, this time from my aunt. Jim read it aloud. "Dad says you have some news. What is it?"

"Oh, this could be fun," Jim said. "Guess!" he said as he typed.

We smirked at each other as the three little dots appeared.

*You're getting married?*

*No, try again.*

*You're moving?*

*No, try again.*

*You're having a baby? LOL.*

Jim and I looked at each other and burst out laughing. A big smile spread across Jim's face. He started typing.

*Not anymore, but she once was.*

We laughed.

Silence from the other end.

Jim sent the photo we had taken a few minutes earlier.

Then the three little dots started up again. We looked up at each other and waited.

After a few minutes, a text came through. *Oh! Is that your daughter with your high school girlfriend?*

Jim's jaw dropped, and he looked at me in shock.

I grinned. "So did everyone know except you?"

Can you imagine, being so young and having such an experience? And then thirty-three years later, you learn that not only is she real but that your brother is sitting face to face with that baby, all grown up.

"I think I have a photo!" she continued.

"A photo?" Jim tipped his head. "What is she talking about?"

"I don't know," I said, still laughing. "I'm new here!"

Fifteen minutes later, my newfound aunt sent over a small hospital photo of a baby. Sure enough, that baby in the photo was me. But it got better.

The photo was torn just right to be the missing photo from the sheet of baby pictures of me that Karen had showed me two weeks earlier. Over thirty-three years later, Jim's sister still had that torn out picture of me. Not only that, but she knew exactly where it was, for such a moment as this.

*Particular people.*
*Particular purpose.*
*Particular time.*

My aunt and birth father exchanged a few messages, and it turns out that in 1983, Karen's sister had shared study hall with Jim's sister. During study hall one day, after I was born, Karen's sister had leaned over to Jim's sister and passed her a small photo of me, from the hospital, and said, "That's your niece."

This was just so unbelievable. Everyone seemed to know. There were photos passed between families, but most of all, what I noticed was that there was acceptance from every single person. Not once was there push back or rejection.

## Redeemed

Remembering God's faithfulness for His people in the Bible helps us trust in His faithfulness for His people in the present. Time and time again, from Genesis to Revelation, we see God continue to love His people. No matter how sinful their acts, how many times they reject Him, we see God continue to love and redeem them. All they did, and all we have to do, is turn to Him.

Sitting in that quiet booth at Panera late on a Friday night, I realized that God was not just redeeming me, answering my prayers to find my birth family, but He was redeeming Jim too. A thirty-three-year-old secret, kept in silence, was now out in the open. God was restoring what Jim had thought to keep private, bringing it out in the open, freeing him from the burden of carrying around the secret any longer.

When we struggle to carry the weight of our past, God keeps showing up. He provided for us in the past and will walk with us throughout our lives. We are witnessing God making a way to redeem our pasts, together in harmony with one another. I had never seen such movement by God in my life. I knew He was with me always, but I hadn't recognized such tremendous movement across multiple people, preparing so many hearts for a series of powerful and healing moments like He had brought together in this moment, right here. I think I was just as much in awe of how God had orchestrated this entire process, for all of us, as I was with the actual events of meeting my birth parents.

Because I could see how clearly the Lord had prepared the hearts of Karen, Lynda, Kyle, Grandpa Jim, and Lynn and Jim, I trusted that He could continue to prepare the hearts of the people I had yet to meet. While I felt euphoric about meeting Karen and Jim so far, being able to grasp how God had planned this for us in advance gave me a great deal of comfort that He would clear the way for those I had not yet met. I trusted God that He would keep Jim's heart and mind open to meeting again. It gave me hope that I might one day meet Lynn, my siblings, and the rest of these new relatives that I had uncovered.

## Saying Goodbye for the First Time

The rest of the evening, we shared photos and stories. I showed him my childhood photos, pictures from proms, and pictures of my kids. I told him about my husband and how we met. About our children and their interests. About my life and what it was like. He shared the same. I was so interested in my siblings and what they were like. I was careful not to ask to meet them. I was sensitive to their ages and what they had been through, having lost their mother only eighteen months prior. As it turned out, they'd lost their mother about the time I'd started looking for Karen. Jim and I acknowledged that that previous timing would have been much different for him and my siblings. God's timing was certainly with us. There was absolutely a reason that it had not worked out before, and we both saw it clearly.

As Panera was preparing to close, I packed up my photos. We walked out of the restaurant together and stood in the parking lot. I did not want to leave. I wondered, no matter how good this meeting had been, if it would happen again. So many stories of other adoptees meeting their parents went well, but then one person panicked and the contact stopped.

I had felt such a strong emotional connection to Jim right away that now I was nervous, self-aware that my emotions were strong. You know the feeling, where you get what you always wanted, whether it is peace, joy, love, or happiness, only to worry that you will lose it? That was exactly the doubt that crept into my heart, standing in the dark in the parking lot, not really wanting to move for fear I wouldn't feel that way again.

We hugged again and joked about how we were both much stronger than we must have known for making it through our entire first meeting without shedding any tears. After a few nervous laughs and a parting goodbye, we walked through the parking lot to our respective vehicles. We had parked just a few spots apart.

As I climbed into my SUV, I put my bag, full of the pictures and albums I had shared, onto the passenger seat. I set my phone in the cup holder and pushed the ignition to turn on the car. My hands were moving, going through the steps to drive, but my mind was in shock. My heart was overflowing. I felt out of sync between my body, heart, and mind. I sat in the driver's seat, waiting for Jim to back out of his parking spot, just a few over from mine. As he pulled away, I put my vehicle in reverse and backed out. As I shifted into drive, my hearted shifted too, and the tears I had unknowingly been holding back dripped down the smile still firmly planted on my face.

## Reflection

*Questions*

1. Do you believe God's love is for you? Why or why not?

2. What are some memories that had a profound impact on who you are?

3. What made those moments significant? How did they shape you? Do you think God was a part of those experiences?

*Affirmations*
1. My sins are redeemed in Jesus.
2. God's plan for me is good.
3. God is teaching me through my experiences.

# chapter thirteen

## HE MADE A WAY

*Lord, you are my God;*
*I will exalt you. I will praise your name,*
*For you have accomplished wonders,*
*Plans formed long ago with perfect faithfulness.*
Isaiah 25:1 CSB

As I PULLED INTO MY NEIGHBORHOOD, my phone vibrated. Jim had messaged me. I was clearly not the only one in awe of what God had done to bring us together. In Jim's words, *It's really a miracle everything that had to happen and go just right for us to be here today . . . I'm so excited to get to know you. Dad.*

The tears that had slowed came back even harder now. I was overwhelmed with the love and kindness that both Karen and Jim had shown me in just a few weeks. I knew God was up to something, bringing us together like this.

I was overcome with emotion, having never been so aware of being a part of God's plan. I had seen God move in my life before through small things, like answering a simple prayer, and had seen His work getting me somewhere safely just in time. However, I had never felt the conviction of His movement like I did through this experience. It was extraordinarily clear it was no coincidence God had timed this reunion just so, for all of us.

### The Tapestry

Have you ever looked at a tapestry? I mean, really looked at it? The top of the tapestry is usually a beautiful, ornate, wonderfully detailed pattern. Each thread is intentionally placed in the exact right spot, in the right sequence, to make a beautiful design. Yet if you flip it over and look at the back side, it's full of knots and seemingly random thread lines, as if there was no pattern or plan to how the tapestry was made. Isn't that the perfect metaphor for life?

As I drove the rest of the way home, I reflected back on the path to get to this place. At all the points where I had either searched for my birth parents, or where Karen had searched for me, there were major events happening in our collective lives that would have made the timing far less than ideal for a happy reunion. It was clear as day that God's hands were on the exact timing. His preparation of our hearts and the way in which it all unfolded was carefully planned. As Paul wrote in Ephesians 1:11 (NLT), "For he chose us in advance, and he makes everything work out according to his plan." I had never seen God's perfect plan so clearly in any other moment of my life. This perspective, seeing it laid out like this, set my faith and my fairly new-found gospel-centered identity on fire. If I had any doubts about God's plans in our lives, they were gone.

Thirty-three years earlier, two imperfect yet chosen teenagers had surrendered a child for adoption. They were both broken in their own way, like every one of us. In 2002, when I turned eighteen, Karen began searching for me. If she had found me then, if I'm honest, there's no way I would have been in the right frame of mind or the right heart space to accept her into my life. At that time, my father was dying of cancer. Every free moment I had I was either spent at school and school activities or grieving the loss of his health. He passed away in 2003, when I was nineteen.

When Karen registered with the International Soundex Reunion Registry in 2007, I was newly engaged, planning a wedding, moving, changing jobs, and had just purchased my first house with my fiancé, now husband. In the midst of that period of my life, I don't think I was ready to meet my birth parents. Until I learned about the letter in 2010, I hadn't really desired to find or meet them.

Everything changed when I learned about the letter. The narrative I had been told, that my father hadn't been involved and that my birth mother wanted to relinquish her rights, didn't drive a desire to search. Yes, I knew I was adopted. My parents had always ensured I knew that. But until I knew about the letter, the desire to find them wasn't there. Had I been able to find my birth parents in 2010, Jim was just getting divorced. I can't imagine me showing up in his life at that point would have been well received, nor would the timing have been good for my siblings, given they were so young. The more recent search in 2016 would have been bad timing for Jim and my siblings as well, for they were grieving the loss of their mother. The Lord laid out His plan and wove it together in a perfect way. Parts of which I am certain we will never fully recognize or appreciate, no matter how much we map out or review the timing of His plan for bringing us all together.

The timing of my mom sharing the letter with me, although I was upset at the time that I hadn't been told sooner, was so important for everything to work out the way in which it did. Had she shared the letter with me at any other time, the outcome wouldn't have been the same. I suspect she might be the most surprised of all to see how God used her to trigger the blessings for all of us to experience. God worked in each one of us to make this happen.

Like the tapestry, God has intentionally placed each of us in our exact spot to make His world just how He needs it to be. The back of the tapestry is messy and tangled, just like our lives. It does not mean the image of the tapestry is broken. It's exactly the way it is supposed to be. Just like you. Just like me.

Perfectly imperfect behind the scenes.

Outwardly put together beautifully, for everyone to see.

Looking underneath the tapestry of life is messy. It's full of mistakes and knots. But if you could see your life the way God does from the mistakes to the knots, something beautiful has emerged. But here's the key point—*we have to do our part*. If we don't know God, if we haven't learned what He's done in the past, to know what He is like, His character, and we aren't in a relationship with Him, then we won't know when He guides us. If I hadn't turned my identity over to the Lord, read His Word, and grown near to Him, then I would not have trusted the nudges I felt to take that DNA test. I would not have trusted the nudges to mail it so quickly. I wouldn't have mailed that reunion registry form, and I certainly wouldn't have tracked down my birth parents so quickly. If it were up to me, I would have spent far more time—months—thinking through each step, carefully evaluating each possible outcome, and nervously deciding what to do.

I would not have found them right here and right now.

His timing is perfect.

But we have to do our part too. We have to lean in and trust Him.

## Deepening the Roots

I pulled into the driveway and parked in the garage. Turning off the engine, I paused before going inside. What a day. Jim was still texting me. It was clear that we had a lot more ground to cover to get to know each other. Karen, too, had been reaching out to me throughout the week.

I briefly gave David the highlights from the night. He mentioned Olivia was waiting up for me and wanted to know how it went tonight with her new grandpa. Just hearing David tell me that brought a big smile to my face. My kids had new grandparents to meet and get to know someday. As I was walking up the stairs to her room, I couldn't help but think what a beautiful blessing it was for them to have more people in their life to love them. I knew they didn't fully understand the significance of what was happening, but someday they would. Especially Olivia, who would remember meeting her grandparents for the first time. William was far too young to remember a time without knowing them.

After tucking Olivia into bed and telling her what it was like to meet my birth father, I lay in bed processing all that had happened. My phone buzzed again, and I ended up exchanging messages with Jim for over an hour. Our conversation pivoted to our respective faith journeys. I had never felt like God was more active in my life than the last six weeks that I had been searching for Jim and Karen, and I shared that with him. There was no other period when He'd carried me through and made something so complicated feel so clear and moved mountains to enable me to realize a dream so quickly. Jim shared that he was in a rough spot spiritually and that this experience had sparked his faith.

*There's no way for me to look at you and not see Him,* he texted.

The tears came rolling back.

*His hand in all of this happening. I've literally had goose bumps driving to work listening to the same Christian music I normally do. Thinking about all that had to align for today to happen.*

Jim was having the same realization I'd had just thirty minutes earlier.

*I don't know how to explain this or say it, but I feel like there's more to His plan than this, which is hard for me to comprehend, given all that's happened in the last 3-4 weeks,* I texted.

Jim told me he trusted I was right about that. What more could there be? I had just met my birth parents after thirty-three years. Wasn't that the big *aha*? I wasn't sure what else God could possibly have planned for us. But I could feel this was part of God's plan to use me for His purpose. I had been praying for God to reveal His purpose for my life for a while. I believed this was the beginning, and I was watching it unfold right in front of me.

## Overcome

I'd cried so many tears the past week that I wasn't sure I would ever stop crying over this. Not because I was sad or happy necessarily—I was just so overcome. Looking back, I am certain that it was the Holy Spirit filling me up, filling us all up, as we were experiencing His presence throughout the reunion.

I was amazed. I didn't deserve this. I'd had a wonderful upbringing. I'd had two loving parents who raised me to be strong, independent, focused, and caring toward others. I had an amazing husband and two beautiful and smart children. I had wonderful in-laws. I did not deserve to *also* have these additional, wonderful people in my life and get to call them family too. It seems like I'd received more than I deserved.

That's the thing with grace, it's a gift—a gift that's unearned, unmerited, for each of us. We have a gracious God Who gives us beautiful experiences when we least expect them.

Despite my overwhelming urge to stop here and to stop the momentum and simply enjoy the relationships that were forming, I recognized the nudge God was giving me. This was not the end. There was more to come from this reunion. How though, God? When there was so much joy and blessing from this already, what else could there possibly be? My heart was already overflowing with both the joy and peace of the reunion, but also the overwhelm of His presence in planning all of this for us.

However, I knew this was not up to me. I know that God's plans are perfect and that it is our job, as His children, to say yes. To obey and to take each step faithfully. At that moment, sitting on the edge of my bed that night, I chose to trust Him. I would keep leaning into His plan. I would have faith to trust God and whatever would come from this point forward.

I accepted that God's plan was better than whatever I could possibly come up with on my own. I accepted that His plan would always be first, and I committed to the Lord that whatever would come from here, whatever His plan, that I would faithfully be His hands and feet.

## Open Heart

From this point forward, I let my expectations go. I stopped trying to figure out what the path forward would look like, how our relationships would form, and what I should *do*, and I simply let God lead. I took each day with an open heart and an open mind, and I consulted with God along the road.

I didn't know why God had decided to bring such healing to my life. When I, a sinner, strayed from Him over and over again, why did He choose me? Why me, Lord?

Why me when there are so many adoptees, so many other people searching desperately for their identity? So many other people searching for this reunion? It didn't seem fair. It didn't seem like I deserved this kind of blessing. I didn't feel worthy.

He reminded me of the love God showed Israel through the prophet Isaiah. No matter how much the people of Israel rebelled against the Lord, He firmly reminded them of their disobedience, but He loved His people anyway. In Isaiah 1:2–20, God tells His people that although He has brought them up, they continue to rebel. He pours out His heart through Isaiah, asking them why they keep rebelling against Him (just like we do today). He urges His children to stop rebelling and that if they are willing to stop, He will give them goodness. Even though the people of Israel continued to rebel, God loved them and kept showing them the right path.

I'd kept rebelling against God. But He'd kept loving me and kept showing me the right path. I was and am so far from God's glorious standards, but He showed me through the reunion with my birth parents that drawing near to Him could lead to goodness. Drawing near to Him and knowing Him, knowing His Word and following His path led me here, to a place of blessing. This reflection encouraged me to keep close to Him, to keep listening, keep following, and keep turning to Him. His love for me—His love for us—will keep us on the right path. His plans for us are rooted in His deep love.

## Reflection

### Questions

1. Have you ever had a time in your life where you felt like something was about to change? How did you handle that change juncture?
2. How might you place your faith in God when you find yourself at a turning point?
3. Who in your life might be a good person to guide you through a turning point?

### Affirmations

1. I can trust God during good times.
2. I can trust God in bad times.
3. I can trust God has me covered always.

# chapter fourteen

## RELUCTANCE

*What shall we say about such wonderful things
as these? If God is for us, who can ever be against
us? Since he did not spare even his own Son
but gave him up for us all, won't he also give us
everything else?*
Romans 8:31–32 NLT

THE NEXT DAY JIM SAT DOWN with his kids Jenna and
Nate separately and explained they had another sibling. He started with Jenna and told her he had been contacted by a woman on Facebook and that person claimed
to be his daughter. He walked her through what had happened to him in college, having been contacted by an attorney to sign over rights for a child—me. He explained
that all these years he hadn't been totally sure he was the
father, even though he had signed the papers because of
the way the attorney had treated him. From what he could

remember, he was pressured to sign the papers. But it was a bit fuzzy given it was so long ago.

He told Jenna a little bit about me and that he had just met me the night before. He was right—Jenna did want to meet me right away. He repeated the same conversation with Nate with similar results.

He asked me if I would be willing to meet them. Of course I wanted to meet my siblings! I'd just met Kyle, my half brother on Karen's side, a week prior, and it was wonderful. Never before did I expect to have siblings anywhere near Jenna's, Nate's, or Kyle's ages. I'd wanted siblings all my life, and now at thirty-three years old, my dream came true. I had a new brother who was three years younger than me, and now a brother and sister who were about half my age.

Despite the age difference, Jenna, Nate, and I had one thing in common: we'd both lost a parent at a young age. Although it's not the most optimistic or happy thing to bond over, it is something that only a few people at a young age have in common. It's a grief most people don't understand until they've been through it.

Jenna and Nate were both involved in sports, were focused in school, and had lots of friends. Seeing the pictures Jim sent, I was filled with love and pride that they were so smart, so kind, and seemed to be thriving despite having been through the loss of their mother just a few years earlier. They were clearly so strong, and I was already so proud of them. I knew what kind of strength it took to get through that kind of a loss. I knew it was hard to put on a brave face every day while you're still grieving. But they were doing it. I was eager to meet them.

I asked Jim what his thoughts were about how it might work. Since we had clearly been going to the same church for at least as long as we had been attending, about three years, Jim thought it might work to meet there. We were going to go to church Sunday evening at our normal time, so we agreed to come a little early so I could meet my siblings.

That afternoon I was nervous. What would my teenage siblings think of their thirtysomething sister? Would we have anything in common besides having been through a similar life experience? What would we talk about? How uncool was I really? I laughed at this notion, but truly, what could we have in common? Would we get along? Would they accept me?

We loaded into the car and drove the twenty-five minutes to church. We parked and headed toward the entrance. Because we attend a large church and there were a lot of places to meet, we'd landed on the atrium. I drew in a big breath and opened the door for my kids. We entered as the sun shone behind us. The large atrium separated The Bridge, a big common room where we had community meals and met for small groups. It was situated between the coffee shop and bookshop, nursery, and worship center.

As we walked through the entry, I could see three people sitting together in the black leather chairs along the perimeter. I could make out that one of the three was Jim, and I could hear him faintly say "that's her" from a distance. As we strode toward them, a teenage girl with long brown hair jumped up from her seat and loped toward me, beaming ear to ear. She walked right up to me, and I gave her a huge hug. To my surprise she hugged me just as tightly. I choked back a few tears and held her close. It was so special, getting to meet her. Next I hugged my littlest brother, Nate. Of all my newfound siblings, I felt like we shared the closest resemblance. At thirteen he seemed so young, yet was clearly so sweet.

My kids were over the moon and so excited to meet their new grandpa, aunt, and uncle. Jenna immediately whisked my kids off to the café to buy them snacks for worship.

I looked in awe at Jim. My kids bubbled with energy. Since I am so much older, I had no idea if meeting Jenna and Nate might be awkward. I was so happy, elated, that this was quite the opposite. What a delightful welcome. My heart was full.

After the service, we sat together in the same black leather chairs, chatting and getting to know one another. An old friend walked up to say hello with her son and looked expectantly at my birth father and my siblings. I had the absolute pleasure of introducing them.

"This is my . . . this is my Jim," I said. I hesitated, nearly having said "dad." That didn't quite feel right. I had a dad. I didn't know how to describe Jim yet.

"And this is my brother Nate and my sister, Jenna."

Tears welled in my eyes. I looked at Nate, who was beaming.

"Yeah!" he exclaimed. "I'm her brother!" So matter of fact.

We all laughed. Nate's excitement cut down my worries about feeling accepted and connected. This was going to be okay.

We soon had to part ways, and I told Jim I hoped to see him again soon.

Each parting left me hanging in the balance. While I yearned to keep this new relationship going, I didn't want to get my hopes up too far. I knew from the other reunion stories that some started out strong and then fizzled. The thought popped into my head, and I immediately shut it down. I didn't come this far to let the Enemy kill my joy. We were just going to take this one step at a time and let our relationships grow.

## But One

The only person who hadn't reached out to me was Lynn, Jim's girlfriend. I had received messages and/or phone calls from three new aunts, grandparents, siblings, and both birth parents. I didn't know what to make of it. On one hand, perhaps that was to be expected; it's not like there are guidelines for how to get to know your boyfriend's new adult child, who just showed up in his life. But on the other hand, I felt anxious. Perhaps she was unsupportive, or at least shocked. I knew she was important to Jim and that he was deeply in love with her. I knew if she was uncomfortable that no matter how much I wanted to keep the relationship with Jim, I would yield to her. I would step back and respect their relationship above all else. I prayed for the discernment to know how to handle this situation and that God would guide us. I prayed for Lynn and for God to open her heart to me and my family. I prayed that she could understand and be open-minded to us.

## Processing

Later that night I told David I felt strongly that I needed to sign up for the Core offered at Hope. Core was a three-part class that explored gospel identity, our role in God's story, and discipleship. There was a new session starting the following week, and I had this indescribable feeling that I was supposed to be there. Even though I had no time to take the class, given I was working full-time and finishing up the last semester of an executive MBA program, I felt that the class would help me process all that was happening. In short, I felt nudged.

We weighed the pros and cons, reviewed the schedule, and decided we could make it work. The next Sunday we drove two cars to church, and I stayed behind after our evening service for class. I walked over to the kiosk, checked in, paced to my assigned table, and introduced myself to the other women at the table.

During dinner, I noticed that there was another small group at the table next to us with women my age. I thought it was odd that I was at a table with women older than me. I speculated that the women at the table next to us were all in their thirties, whereas the women at my table were in their fifties and sixties. I knew the church normally placed groups together based on demographics, but also prayed over the groups and adjusted accordingly. I assumed there was a reason I was with this group and trusted God was at work in this somehow. After the meal ended, we sang a few worship songs with the other classes happening at the same time as Core. As they dismissed the groups, the Cores headed to our room for teaching and small-group time.

Bev, our small-group leader, wanted us to get to know one another better, since none of us knew each other. She asked us to introduce ourselves to share briefly about our faith journey. We went around the table one by one. When it came to my turn, I explained I hadn't grown up in a Christian home but that I'd always believed in God, even as a child, and I'd known that Jesus was a part of Christianity, but I hadn't really understood religion until I was much older. I shared when my father was dying, he would read the Bible with his best friend, and that sparked my interest. I had started going to church in college, and that was when I'd accepted Jesus as my Savior. My faith had slowly grown for about six years until we found our way to Lutheran Church of Hope, where I'd learned more about a relationship with God, and my faith had taken off.

I paused and waited for someone to speak next.

"You know, perhaps the purpose in your father's illness and his passing was to bring you to Jesus. Perhaps God used the hurt and pain of his cancer and death to save you," said Julie, the woman to my right.

I suddenly felt warm all over, and goose bumps formed on my arms. I teared up.

"I have never thought about it that way before," I said. "I guess that's very possible. Had he not been sick, I'm not sure he would have been reading the Bible, and if he hadn't been reading the Bible, I don't know that we would have ever had a conversation about faith."

"I think that's the answer right there, Wendy. I think that's how God used your Dad's illness for good. What a blessing for him to have been able to do that for you in his dying days," Julie continued.

I was fighting back tears now. "You know, his last time in church before he died was for my baptism. It was emotional for me and for him. He cried most of the time," I shared. It was so true. It was his last time in a suit, his last time in a church, and he'd held my hand tightly after my baptism. I'd never seen him so emotional in his life, and I would never see him so emotional on this side of heaven again. He passed away just two and a half months later.

"With regard to why Core, and why now," I continued, "I recently went through a pretty incredible life experience, and I felt like I needed to take Core right now so I can better process everything that's happening. In short, I found some new family members, and it's been powerful and overwhelming. It's not at all convenient for me or my family for me to be here, but I just felt like I needed to sign up right now."

The next activity was to spend a little time reflecting on the topic of creation and answering the question, What are some significant events in your childhood that made you feel safe, secure, invited into something bigger, and that you belong? This was a big question for me. There were a lot of options, but given the changes that had just occurred, I felt like focusing on my adoption made the most sense.

I wrote, "I was adopted as an infant. This made me feel safe and invited into something bigger because it meant that I had two loving people in my life, perhaps more so than they realized at the time, that cared enough about me to give me up for a better life. A life they could not provide. It also meant that I had two people who desperately wanted a child in their life and would take a child, not of their own flesh and blood, into their home and hearts and love me unconditionally, as if I were their own. I always felt very safe, very loved, and very special—like I had extra love in my life, which is never a bad thing."

I shared this reflection and mentioned that I had recently found my birth parents and that the experience led me to sign up for Core. Part of the reason was so I could dig into my emotions, when normally I may have tried to tuck them away to deal with later.

Julie asked me if I had met them and if I had started to form any kind of a relationship with them. I said that I had met both my birth mom and birth dad and that I had a relationship with both of them. Although very different, it was far more than I'd expected on both sides, but especially with my dad, in part because it was so unexpected.

The conversation continued around the group, and women all had such rich life stories and faith walks. I knew I could learn from them during the class. There was something special about this group of women, and I left that first night feeling like we were going to have a great class.

## Reflection

*Questions*

1. How can you work to grow your faith?
2. What might happen if you choose to go deeper or wider in your relationship with the Lord?
3. Do you have a faith community to lean on? If not, where might you meet others with strong faith to learn from?

*Affirmations*
1. God will put people in my life to help me.
2. God uses particular people, for particular purposes, at particular times.
3. I am willing to let God use me.

*chapter fifteen*

## PRAYER CIRCLES

*In the same way, the Spirit also helps us in our
weakness, because we do not know what to pray
for as we should, but the Spirit himself intercedes
for us with unspoken groanings. And he who
searches our hearts knows the mind of the Spirit,
because he intercedes for the saints according to
the will of God.*
Romans 8:26–27 CSB

A FEW WEEKS HAD PASSED NOW since I'd met my birth
parents, and we were all learning so much about each
other. My husband and children were regulars at the 5:00
p.m. church service on Sunday evenings, and the last few
weeks Jim had been joining us for that service. I'd never
worshiped with a parent before outside of holidays, so having Jim there with us was special. Our church offered one-
on-one prayer after each service was complete, and anyone

could walk up and receive prayer. Jim asked me if I would be willing to receive prayer over our new relationship after service sometime, and I gladly agreed.

Sunday evening September 17, Jim joined us for the service even though he had already attended church with my brother and sister that morning. I had to choke back tears as the band played the song "Good, Good Father," given how deeply good He had been to us recently. As that band moved on to the final worship song, I looked at Jim and asked him if he was ready to go receive prayer. Although he had been the one to ask me, his eyes told me he was surprised I was ready to go right away. I felt in my heart this would be a good foundation for us, and so why not go now?

He nodded, and we walked over to the prayer-partner line and waited for our turn. When the prayer in front of us ended, we walked up to the first prayer partner, who I recognized from Alpha. Having served in the Alpha ministry at our church, I knew several people who were gifted in prayer and was at ease knowing Jason would be praying for us.

"Hi, Jason!" I set my purse down on the ground and stood expectantly with Jim.

"How can I pray for you?" Jason asked.

I spoke up first. "Well . . ." I paused and smiled at Jim. "This is my biological father, Jim, and we just met three weeks ago. We'd like to have you pray over our relationship and the future for us."

Jim smiled back at me.

"Okay, sure," Jason said. "Can we join hands?"

We all held hands in a circle and bowed our heads. Jason prayed over us, and I let my mind get quiet. He asked God to come around us and help our relationship to grow, to bless it, and to have us keep God at the center. While he was praying, I got this clear image of a white circle. I had never experienced this before—seeing something visually while praying. It was so distinctive, yet I didn't know what it meant. As Jason continued to pray, he made several references to things I had been thinking recently or praying about myself. He talked about growing a relationship from dirt, from the ground up. For nurturing it and allowing it to grow organically over time. He mentioned family trees, which was how I'd found Jim's dad—Grandpa Jim— through our family tree.

While Jason was praying, I continued to see the distinct vision of a bright white light through fog, with a clear open circle in the middle. The circle was even brighter than the light, as if it were radiating. I kept losing focus of the circle and then would get it back in plain view. I had no idea what it meant, but it was present throughout the prayer.

When Jason finished praying over Jim and me, we embraced. It was powerful to feel the love of God wrap around us. There was no doubt the Holy Spirit was there with us in that moment, and if we kept Him in the middle, our relationship would grow into something good. As I was thinking about it, I remembered Jason mentioning the word *good* over and over again, but I couldn't recall exactly what he'd said.

After we let go, we thanked Jason for praying over us. I had my Core after the service, so I walked with Jim, David, and my kids through the worship center and out to the atrium where I had met Nate and Jenna for the first time. We said our goodbyes, and I gave my kids hugs before they left with David to go home.

## Core

I walked over to The Bridge through the atrium. The room was large and open, with a small stage along the south wall. The space was arranged with white plastic square tables and seating for about eight to ten each. The tables had signs on them, indicating which group was to sit where for the Sunday evening classes. All Sunday evening classes at the church start with a meal and conversation, so it was busy and crowded.

I took a last peek at my phone as I walked over to my assigned table.

Jim had texted me. *That was beautiful. Thank you.* I smiled and closed my text messages for dinner. I was full of joy from the prayer time, the image of the circle still swirling in my head.

I sat my bag down and walked over to the line to gather a plate of food and then made my way back to my group's table. Julie was already sitting in the chair next to my bag. After pulling the chair out and moving my bag to the floor, I sat next to her and asked her how her week had been and how she was doing. After exchanging a few words, she asked me how things were going with my newly found birth parents. I let her know things were going well, that we were all still getting to know each other, and that I had just attended service with my birth father immediately before small group. Julie commented about how neat she thought it was that not only were both my birth parents believers but that I had just attended church with my birth father.

After we finished the meal, we were dismissed to walk to The Well room to hear the message for the evening. As we walked downstairs, I shared with Julie about what had happened earlier that night regarding our prayers and how it had unfolded. As we neared our table and sat down, she asked if I looked anything like my birth parents and wondered if I had a picture I could share with her. I reached into my bag and pulled out my phone. Bev had walked up behind us and sat down just as we were settling into our seats.

I leaned over to Julie to share the picture of me with Karen first. Bev looked over her shoulder and commented about how similar our smiles were and how happy we both looked.

"You have the same smile!" Julie remarked. I smiled because it was true. It was still so weird, in the best way, to know family that I looked like.

Bev asked if I also knew my birth father, and I scrolled to find the photo of me with Jim.

"Here's the photo with my birth father from the night we met." I held it up for Julie and Bev to see.

Julie lit up, smiling big. "Wow! You look *so* much like him! You have the same eyes, nose, and smile lines!"

Bev leaned over, and her face lit up. She teared up and looked at me in disbelief.

The color drained from Bev's face. Her jaw dropped.

*Oh no*, I thought. *She knows him. She has to.*

How could I have been so careless to show this to someone not even thinking that Jim might know them too? A sinking feeling came over me. This was the first time I had shared my story with someone I didn't know personally. Of course it would be someone who knew Jim. It was Des Moines. Although it wasn't a small town, it wasn't big either. We'd lived in some of the same areas of town, attended the same church—heck, I'd even bought a car from the dealership he used to work at. He and I had already established that we likely knew some of the same people.

But I was not prepared for that to be in church, in my small group of just seven women. Bev slowly shared through tears that her stepdaughter was Dad's girlfriend (I had decided to call him Dad by then.) Bev's stepdaughter was Lynn.

Yes, *the* Lynn.

Lynn was the one person in all of this who I felt was missing from this whole situation. I didn't know for sure why, but she was the one person who hadn't reached out to me. I had continued to pray for the Lord to soften Lynn's heart toward me for a few weeks, but no change. I had prayed for her acceptance of me and my family and that God would make a path for her to want to get to know me and support Jim and me.

Over the last few weeks, I had felt God nudging me to keep praying for her. I prayed daily. I wasn't praying for her to accept me, because I didn't assume that she (or anyone) would want to meet me. I simply didn't want her to be upset with Jim or cause any problems in their relationship.

## Living Testimony

By this time Bev and I were holding hands with each other across the table and had tears pouring down our faces. The Lord's plan to bring us together in this group for this specific purpose was abundantly clear. I couldn't believe it. I was overwhelmed with the power of God, planning for both of us to say yes to this class and get aligned in this small group and opening both of us to this conversation right here and right now. I knew this was the reason why God had put Core on my heart. He needed me to be there. He was going to use me to break through to Lynn through Bev. He was using Bev and me to show to the rest of our group how the Holy Spirit works.

I was nervous, anxious, scared, overwhelmed, in total awe, and so many other emotions I can't describe. I knew these were human emotions and I needed to trust that the Lord would not lead me down a path to hurt me or hurt any of us through this. I was on my knees with God in this moment. I felt completely in His will. I knew with absolute assurance that He'd orchestrated that very moment. All I needed to do was surrender. I surrendered. I chose to let go and let God. I decided to let God's plans be *the* plan.

Julie was sitting between Bev and me during this powerful moment and had her arms around us both. She also was in tears by this time and shared she felt God had put her in this place for a reason too—so she could witness the Holy Spirit at work. Her comment, that she felt God used me to move her, hit me hard. I have never felt the Lord use me like that before. What an incredible blessing to have God use you for His purpose, especially to testify to His presence. If I ever had a shred of doubt that God was working in my life, He crushed that doubt in that one single moment. It was like having gasoline poured all over the fire of my faith.

## Circles

As Bev, Julie, and I sat together through the rest of the evening, it was clear that this was going to change my life forever. I felt overpowered and consumed by the Lord. I felt like I had been completely filled with the spirit and also hit over the head with a two-by-four at the same time.

I felt broken, down to my absolute core.

I felt filled, overflowing with the Lord's presence.

I was in awe of what He had done.

I was in awe of what He was doing right in the moment.

I was in awe of what He was going to do in the future.

I simply cried. The entire rest of the night, openly, tears flowed down my face, and they didn't stop.

As the pastor stood to start the lesson, Julie, Bev, and I tried to collect ourselves, but it was clear we were going to be distracted. Julie kept whispering how amazed she was to be witnessing this. Bev kept squeezing my hand. I just kept crying.

The evening's lesson was all about the phases of God's grand story: creation, rebellion, resurrection, and restoration. I managed a slight laugh through the tears. What a perfect example of God's story this situation was. We started talking about the beginning, in Genesis 1 and 2, where God created heaven and earth and things were good.

The message focused on the beginning of time and the connection to the creation of our lives being good. The pastor put a slide up on the screen with a symbol representing creation, rebellion, resurrection, and restoration.

Bev immediately looked over at me, her face alight. "Do you see that? Creation is depicted as a perfect circle, and when God created you, it was perfect. That rebellion is represented by a torn circle, and that symbolizes you being split away from your birth parents." My heartbeat quickened, and tears streamed down my face again.

Julie looked at me and said, "This message is glowing through you. Your face is absolutely filled with His glory."

## Renewal

She was right. In the beginning of my life, and the beginning of your life, things were good. God planned for us, He created us, and things were good. But then something bad happened, some kind of rebellion. In the Bible, Adam and Eve ate from the tree, and thus rebelled against God. In the same way, my original family unit was also broken. I was conceived by two teen parents who'd relinquished me for adoption. My parents wanted a child and could not have one on their own. When God split me from my birth parents, He planned to fill my adoptive parents' hearts, knowing one day He would bring us all together.

Even though I knew I was planned for, created with purpose, split apart, and reunited, seeing this in clear black and white, tightly aligned to the gospel, it was as if I was seeing it all for the first time. It was so plainly outlined in front of me as a part of the lesson, and Bev was right here telling me the exact words I needed and speaking them into my soul. I felt paralyzed. I was amazed by God's work.

The next hour was a blur. I alternated between trying to take notes and trying to stop crying. Julie leaned over and put her arm around me again and reminded me that if there was a safe place to let it out, to cry, this was it.

She was right. This was a safe place to have a breakthrough.

We continued through the teaching, walking through creation to restoration. I wrote notes about the fractured relationship between me and my birth parents, about my adoption, and about the reunion being separate restorations.

Any shred of doubt I had that God was behind this reunion was completely removed from my heart. I pulled out my phone and sent Jim a text. I needed to give him the heads-up that Bev knew about me and was witness to a powerful night. God had used her to help me process what was happening around us. I'd felt compelled to sign up for a class called Core because I felt like it would help me process what was happening. I never expected it to be so powerful. I guess there was no holding the secret of me in now.

*So you'll never believe this*, I typed. *Bev is my Core leader.*

*Who's that?* he responded.

*Lynn's stepmom?*

*WTH! Didn't register. WOW! He's showing off again!* Jim texted.

*I'll text you more afterward. I hope I didn't put you in a bad spot. I'm very sorry if I did. It wasn't my intention at all.*

I knew this wasn't the end of the power of the evening.

There was still more to come. I slipped my phone back into my bag as class continued. I was shaken to my core. There was nothing I could do now. Bev was witness to all of this, and now I had to trust that God would guide her with Lynn.

## Reflection

### Questions

1. Think about a time you had a powerful experience. Why was it so powerful?
2. How did the experience change you? Do you think it could happen again? Why or why not?
3. Consider sharing that powerful experience with a friend or family member you trust. Share how and where God was a part of that experience.

### Affirmations

1. Even when things seem hard, God is with me.
2. When things are good, God is with me.
3. When I turn to Him, He will carry me through.

# *chapter sixteen*

## RESTORATION

*Blessed is the man who remains steadfast under
trial, for when he has stood the test he will
receive the crown of life, which God has promised
to those who love him.*

James 1:12

As the pastor wrapped up his talk, he showed a video of a single song he felt tied the message together. As the lights dimmed and the screen glowed, I knew what was coming—the song that had felt like the anthem to my entire experience of finding my birth parents—"No Longer Slaves" by Bethel Music. Tears welled up in my eyes. This time I didn't fight them; I let them flow with the melody of the song. I closed my eyes and let the tears drop one by one. I thought back to all that had happened to bring us all together.

I thought back to what happened the last two months, and the same few songs kept coming up, almost like a soundtrack for the experience. Even though the songs were not new to me, they moved me in ways they never had before—no matter how many times I had heard or sang them. Now, the introductory note to this song was enough to move me to tears.

Music had always served as something I could relate to—that I could find peace and comfort in. These same few songs seemed to be surrounding me with comfort that the Lord knew my heart and knew what I was experiencing, and it was good.

As the song played, I reflected. I had been so worried this experience would not be good and would be painful or terrible or that some bad would come from it. But, as the song mentioned, the enemies of that worry, the doubt (which isn't of God, because God brings *good* out of bad experiences—He does not bring us bad experiences) had been removed. Each potential roadblock had been removed at each juncture. Just as soon as I'd surrendered it all over to God, the goodness flowed like a raging river.

All my fears were gone. Completely gone.

I prayed as the song continued. I no longer had to be a slave to the fear of the unknown, of the possibilities of where I came from or who my parents are. Because of God, I had the answers I was seeking. I had both the firmness of my identity rooted in the truth of God's Word, as well as the answers to my origin. None of this experience would have been possible without God.

Now more than ever I can see how my surrender to

Him was required before He could show me the answers to what I had been seeking. It is through Him that all things were and are possible. It is through the Lord that I was able to find the information, the people, and the wholeness I had longed for.

Despite the circumstances surrounding my birth, God chose me to be in this world for a purpose. The story around my purpose—why God brought me into this world—was unfolded around us at this moment. While I didn't know what the future held, I was so aware of His presence in my life and the lives of those in this experience. I knew there was more to come from this, and instead of being nervous or scared, for the first time ever, I felt complete peace. Complete trust in Him and His plan for me. I surrendered.

I thought about the concept of family. Here I was, thirty-three years old, and reflecting deeply on what made a family, a family. As Paul wrote in Ephesians 1:5, "God decided in advance to adopt us into his own family by bringing us to himself through Jesus Christ." I felt like I was understanding this verse for the first time. God had decided in advance. He decided in advance to create us, to create you, and to create me. God chose to adopt us into His family, the same way my parents had adopted me into their family. Yet here, thirty-three years later, I was understanding the significance of family for the first time. I'd found the meaning of family.

What makes a family, a family anyway? Is it blood? Is it rituals? Laughter? A simple memory of something in the past? Hope for the future? Or perhaps it is simply the bond of time. Time spent together on this earth, focused on Him. If you had asked me four months ago what made a family, family, I would have had a very different perspective. In that moment, with tears flowing down my face, surrendering, I could see that family is a much broader term. It is all those things: rituals, laughter, memories, all connected through love. But most importantly, connected through the blood of Jesus. Families are complicated, yet so simple. Family is found in many ways, through many different paths, but always formed through God's plan. The feeling of connectedness to family now that I've drawn near to God is far stronger than I ever expected.

I was restored to God. I was restored with my adoptive parents. I was restored with my birth parents. All was restored.

It seemed so ridiculous now that I had been so worried about this path. God had guided the entire process, and it was so clear that all I had to do was trust Him. All we have to do is trust Him.

The last piece of the puzzle was Lynn's acceptance. I knew she meant the world to Jim, and I would never want to impact their relationship. I was so afraid that Jim, especially, would reject me. I had read so many stories of rejection, especially from birth fathers. When I'd first reached out to Jim, I'd been expecting the worst. I didn't know much about him, only that he had not been involved in my birth. I expected to have to attempt to contact him in a few ways, a few times, just to try to convince him to give me the medical information I'd been seeking. Instead he responded so open and kindhearted—he'd welcomed me into his life with open arms and love. Unconditional love I could have never expected.

I am still so amazed and thankful for God's work in Jim's life and his heart to accept me so openly into the life of his family. He didn't reject me. He accepted me.

This whole experience had already surpassed any of my wildest dreams and transformed my faith forever. I had to surrender this last piece to the Lord. He had planned all the goodness to this point. Why would He stop now?

As the song ended and the lights came up, my tears slowed but didn't stop. I was a fool to think this was the end. There was clearly much more in store. I opened my eyes and whispered, "I surrender, Lord. I surrender to You. Your will be done. I trust You."

## Healing

Bev reached over and gently touched my elbow, offering me a tissue. I thanked her, and she leaned closer to whisper in my ear.

"There are big plans here, Wendy. Why don't we pray together after this? I'll grab a prayer partner to pray with us."

"Sure," I whispered back. "I need to pick up my daughter from the nursery, and then I'll come back and meet you here."

After the closing remarks, I went to pick up Olivia and then came back to The Well to pray with Bev and Scott, the leader of the prayer team. When we sat down with Scott, I explained to him that I had recently found and met my birth father, who also attended Hope Lutheran. We had just spent the evening at worship together and received prayer over our relationship following the service. I shared that Bev and I had uncovered our connection and we both felt strongly that it was no accident we were placed in the Core group together. I also asked that we pray for Lynn, Bev's stepdaughter, and that the Lord would bless her in this process as well. We were all connected to what the Holy Spirit was doing in our lives, even though we didn't fully understand how or to what extent.

Before we prayed, Bev said very matter of fact, "I'm here in her place. That's why God put me here. There's a reason for this."

I was speechless. I had no idea where Lynn's heart was or how she was feeling, since I hadn't had any contact with her. At that moment, Scott, Bev, and I joined hands in a circle, and Scott prayed over our relationship. He praised God for His works and for bringing us all together. During the prayer I marveled at the connectedness and continued symbolism throughout the evening. Good. Circle. Connectivity. Love. Scott prayed and we cried. Olivia came to me at one point during the prayer and put her arms around my shoulders and her head against mine.

"Mommy, don't cry," she said, which only made my tears flow faster.

Scott closed the prayer, and we all opened our eyes. We were all in tears.

"Wow," Bev said. "That was beautiful, Scott. I'm so amazed. Wendy, this is so good. There is such a goodness here. I can feel it."

I thanked her for leaning into this situation and praying with me. What a blessing it was to have her here with me tonight, to help me better understand the connection of the lesson and my creation, to walk through this lesson on rebellion, resurrection, and restoration, and to pray for our family's future. We shared a big hug and parted ways.

Walking to my car with Olivia, I texted Jim. I let him know I had just finished praying with Bev and that I would be surprised if Bev didn't immediately call Lynn.

By the time I got home, I had managed to pull it together. I think I had run out of tears to shed. I put Olivia to bed and then sat down to process. I checked my phone to see Jim's message, that he was headed to meet up with Lynn. It all made sense now, why praying for Lynn had been on my heart. While there had been no specific reason for that, at least that I was aware of, I had felt compelled to pray for the softening of her heart. And held tightly to faith to trust God's plan.

## Completion

The next morning I had a business trip and was flying to California. While waiting at the gate during my layover, very early in the morning, I received a message request.

From Lynn.

She wanted to meet me. She too was in awe of the work God was doing in our lives, to bring us all together. Again, God had answered my prayers. I told Lynn I would be honored to meet her and would be glad to do so as soon as I returned from my trip. Throughout the week, she sent me sweet stories about Jim, told me how much she cared for him, and sent me several pictures. It was clear that God had us covered.

When we met that Friday night, we bonded easily. She was lovely and had such a positive energy about her. We quickly learned we had a lot in common, and her love for Jim was so clear. It made me so happy to know he was happy. After meeting Lynn, I felt the weight lift. God had answered all our prayers and then some. He blessed us because He loves us.

## Reflection

### Questions

1. How might God answer prayers in ways you don't expect?
2. Can you think of a time when God answered your prayers differently than you expected? What was that like?
3. Describe how God used something unexpected to bless you or someone you know.

### Affirmations

1. God's love for me is sacred.
2. If I ask for God's help, He will answer me in His perfect time.
3. God is always with me.

# *chapter seventeen*

## SURRENDER

*And I am sure of this, that he who began a good
work in you will bring it to completion at the
day of Jesus Christ.*
Philippians 1:6

I SAT SHOULDER TO SHOULDER BETWEEN my aunt Kathy
and my sister, Jenna, on a bench hauled in to my living
room from the kitchen table. A dull roar of voices swept
across the room. As I looked around, first at the glimmer of
the white lights on the Christmas tree and across at all the
family sprawled across the floor, on couches and standing, I
couldn't help but smile. Watching the interaction, hearing
the laugher rippling across the room, and taking it all in, I
couldn't help but be in awe. God was so good. Five months
ago I hadn't know a single person in this room, and now,
on Christmas Eve, I sat surrounded by love. These people,

who I now called family, accepted me wholeheartedly. I would never get over the work the Lord did to create this moment, and so many others. I couldn't believe He did all this for us. He gave us just what we needed at just the right time.

I locked eyes with my dad and noticed he was doing the same thing I was. He was soaking in the profoundness of the moment. Savoring every sound, every laugh, the joy, and feeling the significance. We were forming new memories, new bonds, and fulfilling so many prayers at one moment. It was a moment I would never forget. My heart was overflowing with love and gratitude for all that had to occur to lead to this time. All the mistakes, the sin, the grace, and the restoration that God brought.

Wrapping paper was strewn about among new toys and framed family photos. I caught myself tearing up. For all those years, I'd thought I had been finding family, I had been searching, and that I had been in control. How wrong I had been.

When we come to understand *and accept* God loves us despite our deepest flaws and failures, that He is still crazy about us, and His love for us grounds our entire life, that's when we have really found our family. That's when we find God's family, God's plan for us.

Regardless of our creation.

Regardless of what other people say.

Regardless of what we achieve.

At the sight of my newly found family packed into my living room, I was overcome by a wave of amazement. As if it were the most natural thing in the world, people I had only known a few months were gathered in my home on Christmas Eve—from four states and made up four generations. All that had to happen to make this moment, the years of life events to bring every single one of us to this point, became oh so present.

In that moment, for the first time, I felt like I truly belonged. I was with my family, as my true self, and I felt complete. God had restored what had been broken, and He did it through our love for Him and His love for us.

What restoration do you need?

What has been broken in your life?

Are you walking boldly in faith with God? Or are you trying to do it all on your own?

If I've learned anything from this life-changing experience, it's that by doing things alone, we are missing out on God's grand plan. By walking with Him, things have a way of falling perfectly into place. I developed an understanding, and I realized in that moment, for the first time, just how powerful grace is. Not just for me, not just for my birth parents, but for all of us. No matter what happens in any of our lives, God stitched us together to have all these beautiful memories, in spite of our imperfections, in spite of our earthly creation, and in spite of any feelings of rejection or shame. He brought us together through grace and a plan that only He could orchestrate.

As I looked around that room on Christmas, every single person needed God's grace, and here we stood. Loved. Saved. By God's perfect plan.

## On Earth as It Is in Heaven

Over the next couple of months, a number of blessings continued to flow. Developing relationships with each of my siblings was wonderful and exciting. I got to know them over time, learn about their interests, and include them in family events.

Now, three years later, it's like they've always been here. There are times that are a bit sad, when I think about the time we didn't know each other and the memories we don't have to build on. I missed the firsts they had that we don't share from our childhood—first days of school, birthdays, and graduations. Or when Olivia was born and we didn't know them, so they weren't able to hold her and celebrate those first moments of her life. Or when William was baptized at the very church where so much of this story unfolded. It's very possible they could've been there the day William was baptized, and yet we had no idea we were celebrating Jesus together. It's just mind-boggling we were all around each other, circulating in the same metro area, the same small town of Des Moines, for decades without even knowing it.

When I talked through all the places I lived in the metro area with both Jim and Karen, it was pretty remarkable to see how our lives had crossed paths over and over again, yet we didn't know one another until 2017. With Jim, we actually lived within a few blocks of each other a few different times. I took classes at Des Moines Playhouse, which is right across the street from the high school that Jim and Karen went to in the late 1980s. Since neither one had left Des Moines, who knew how many times we could've crossed paths and not known it.

I met Jim's dad, my Grandpa Jim, the same day he returned to the United States after his trip to Europe. It was so special that he wanted to meet me the very day he returned. Not the next day or the day after, but the same day. I got to meet my grandmother Harriette, along with her husband, Cat, at Christmas.

Yet, with all the blessings, the hardest thing is knowing we were all so close all this time, yet we didn't have those common shared family experiences that drive connection. The hardest for me is the ache of not having them at our wedding. Sharing our wedding album with our new family was special, but I can't help but think about how much I wish they had been there. Nate and Jenna would've been just the right age to be the perfect flower girl and ring bearer. Since my father had passed away, who knows—perhaps I wouldn't have walked myself down the aisle after all.

But God had a plan for a wedding. And it was *very* special. Jim and Lynn got engaged about three weeks after I met Lynn and were married the following April at Lutheran Church of Hope. Guess who got to be the flower girl and ring bearer? Yep. Olivia and William. There has been so much goodness that has come from the timing God planned for us. While I do have moments of sadness that were missed, I am so confident that God's timing is perfect. It was one of the most joyous moments of my life, walking down the aisle with Grandpa Jim, standing next to my siblings and my children, while Jim pledged his heart to Lynn. Bev officiated. Standing at the altar that beautiful April day was clearly part of God's plan.

To this day it is still my instinct to try to do things my way, on my timing. But this profound experience has taught me to stop—to walk with God, to pray, and to rest in the knowledge that God's got this. I can try to fight for what I want, or I can let God build the path before me one step at a time. When things are tough or I feel myself trying to take ahold of the path, I remember what He did for us, and I trust Him.

There is simply no way anyone or anything could have brought this specific collection of moments, with this specific group of people in this specific timing, other than God. Only God could have made this happen in such a short span of time, preparing everyone's hearts and aligning all our lives *just so* we were all prepared to say yes to this reunion.

I remember.

I remember what God did for me, to bring me here.

I remember what God did for my birth parents, to prepare their hearts for this reunion.

I remember what God did for you, to bring you to the place to read this story.

I remember what he did for *us*, to bring us together for this particular moment.

Particular people.

Particular purpose.

Particular time.

This is the business God is in—picking up our pieces, our brokenness, and our sins, and bringing those pieces together, weaving them into a beautiful tapestry—full of knots and mistakes and failures. He has knit each of us into this beautiful reunion, a reunion only He could craft. God brought us all together in His perfect plan, a plan no one else could have orchestrated in no other time, with no other people. God chose us for this redemption story, and He chooses you for your story. Every single day, He chooses you. You don't have to create your own story—God has got you. He created you for a particular purpose, right here and right now. Turn to Him, let go of everything else, and watch what He does in your life.

You never know what you might find.

## The Presence

As Matthew 7:7 (csb) explains, "Ask, and it will be given to you Seek, and you will find. Knock, and the door will be opened to you." I asked for God to show me my purpose, I sought my identity, and I found it rooted in Him. I then asked Him to let me find my biological parents, and the door was most certainly opened for me. Our God restores all things. He restored my identity rooted in Him. He restored thirty-three years of hurt for Karen and Jim. He restored so many other relationships. He paved a path forward for new relationships, new healing, and created this beautiful testimony for us to give of His good works in our lives. In the short three years I've know my new family, each of us has told this story of our reunion many times. The number of people whom this story has blessed is already unquantifiable. God is using us to share His love.

The Holy Spirit was once defined to me as the presence of God in the present tense. It took me a long time to fully understand. It took this experience for me to recognize Him. The Holy Spirit was with me that day in Ohio when

I heard about the AncestryDNA test and felt His nudge to buy it. He was with me when I received my results and found all the right information to quickly identify who my birth parents were. He was with me still when I crafted those first messages and met my birth parents for the first time. He was with me when I explained to my mom that I had found them and asked for her support. He was with me each step of the way.

This book is the testimony of what God did in my life, by me simply saying *yes* to Him. By turning over my identity to the Lord, by following His nudges, and by trusting Him. Looking back, I wonder how many people's lives are impacted by our story beyond Jim, Karen, and me? How many people have different relationships with us or with each other? How many souls are impacted by the testimony of God's works? All because of a simple moment of surrender.

## What If

What would happen if you surrendered to God? What if you placed your identity in Him and not in the things of this world? What if you were to stop placing your identity and purpose in the roles you play and the hats you wear but instead place your life in the arms of the Lord and let Him lead you? *What if you were you and God were God?*

What if.

What if that simple surrender could change everything?

What if.

What if it transforms not only your own life but the lives of those around you?

What if.

What if the Lord's Prayer were to come alive for you?

What if.

What if God's will for you is to have a slice of heaven right here and right now?

What if.

That's what we got. We received our little piece of heaven when He reunited us, used us for His good, and let us live that glory out here and now. As Jesus taught us, *Thy* will be done.

On earth as it is in heaven.

God's will.

Right here.

Right now.

What if.

What are you waiting for?

Let go and let God.

> *With God, all things are possible.*
> Matthew 19:26 CSB

## Reflection

*Questions*

1. What steps can you take to follow God's plan for your life?

2. How do you think about God's timing versus your own?

3. How has your perspective changed since reading this book?

*Affirmations*

1. I am adopted as God's child.
2. I have purpose.
3. I am accepted for who I am, not what I've done.
4. I am chosen.
5. I am predestined.
6. I am redeemed.
7. I am forgiven.
8. I am planned for.
9. I am sealed.
10. I am renewed.
11. I am a new creation.
12. I am His.

# acknowledgments

A T THE TIME THIS BOOK IS going to print, it's now three years after I reunited my birth parents, siblings, grandparents, aunts, uncles, and countless other extended family members. When I reflect upon what happened throughout 2017, I am just as amazed by the hand of God throughout all our lives today as I was when this was unfolding. Writing this book has been equally as powerful as the experience.

First and foremost, thank You, God, for using us to tell this beautiful story of Your love. Through this powerful experience, You used each one of us in a unique way to show the world how You plan our lives in advance. Over the thirty-three years leading up to this experience, You carefully planned the way this would unfold. You prepared our hearts individually to experience such immense and overwhelming love in a way only *You* could create. I feel humbly honored to serve You by sharing with the world, through this book, what You did for us.

To my dad Bill. I miss you every day. I never had the chance to tell you, but in your final days before you passed from this world into the next, seeing you draw near to the Lord and studying the Word, is what led me to Jesus Christ. Seeing you turn to Him turned me to Him. Thank you for modeling the way for me. Your very last time in church before you passed was for my baptism, and I will never forget what you said to me that day. God is proud of you too, Dad. I love you.

To my mom, Tee, thank you for telling me about the letter. This seemingly small detail impacted dozens of people through this experience. Thank you for urging me to track down the letter and for supporting me through forming these new relationships. I love you, Mom. You started a chain of events that impacted many others to hear about God's plan and His love for us. God loves you.

To David, there is no greater cheerleader on this side of heaven than you. Thank you for urging me to take the test, to find my biological family, for supporting me through the writing of His work in our lives, and for loving me fiercely every day. Because of you, so many others will get to hear this story of God's love. You serve the Lord beautifully.

To my children, Olivia, William, and Charlotte. I love you with all my heart. Your identity is far greater than what anyone could possibly say to you. You can't earn it. God has bestowed it upon you. You are chosen by Him. Turn to Him for guidance, love, and acceptance, always. His plans for your precious lives are far greater than any plans you could create yourselves. May you always know who you are in the Lord's eyes.

To Karen, thank you for carrying me, for giving me the life I had by putting me up for adoption. I can't imagine the pain it caused you. God used that pain for such good. Thank you for loving me all my life.

To Jim, thank you for accepting me with open arms and for encouraging me to write this book. I never expected you to respond to those first messages, and I think I can speak for several people when I say, we're so glad you did.

To Lynn, thank you for trusting God that this was good and for listening to Bev's call, and for always including me and my family in everything. Your cooking is legendary around the Batchelder household. Thank you for accepting me.

To Bev, thank you for letting God use you. You have such a beautiful servant's heart for the Lord. You inspire me and so many others to be willing to be the hands and feet of the Lord. You taught me so much about identity and who God says I am. Thank you for helping me accept who I am.

To my siblings, Jenna, Nate, and Kyle, and my stepsiblings, Jordan and Zach—you answered a lifetime of prayers and desire to have siblings. I suspected I had some out there somewhere but never expected to have such a bond with each of you, despite our age differences. You are each so special to me in your own unique way. Keep your eyes fixed on the Lord, and He will guide you always. It's such a blessing to be your sister. I love you so much.

To my aunts: Aunt Erica, thank you for keeping a thirty-three-year-old photo! I cannot tell you how much I enjoyed seeing it and how many laughs Jim and I have had over your ability to find it at a moment's notice. To Aunt

Kathy, thank you for all the stories and for always making time for me. I love our FaceTime calls. To Aunt Lynda thank you for taking the DNA test and for responding to our messages. You were the missing link to Karen.

To Grandpa Jim, Grandma Sandy, Grandma Harriette, and Papa Cat, the world's best secret keepers—thank you for your beautiful messages, your unconditional love, and for embracing me and my family. You are all really special.

To the amazing staff at Lutheran Church of Hope—Mel, Susan, Pastor Mike, Pastor Jeremy, and Pastor Andy—thank you for the wonderful programs you offer. God is using Lutheran Church of Hope in a big, big way. I know my story is *not* unique. Your guidance and teachings through Alpha and Core have changed my life, and so many others, in this one testimony alone. I know there are thousands like this. Thank you for the beautiful way you serve the Lord.

Last and certainly not least, to the Redemption Press team—Cynthia, Dori, Carrie, and Athena—thanks for taking a chance on a first-time author to share the love of Jesus with the world.

# Appendix

**Resources for Adoption Search**

International Soundex Reunion Registry: http://www.isrr.
org/Search.html

Ancestry.com DNA: http://www.ancestry.com/dnaapp

# to my fellow adoptee

I FULLY RECOGNIZE THAT NOT ALL reunion stories have this type of happy ending. I have read and pored over and cried many tears reading the stories of others who did not get the same happy ending that I did. I prayed for this for many, many years. My heart breaks for you and that desire to be accepted by your earthly family.

Please hear me. If we were sitting together, I would wrap my arms around you and whisper this in your ear with the most love and a heap of grace. I urge you to think about why this matters so much to you. What is it that you are searching for? Is it acceptance? Is it answers? If answers, which ones? If acceptance, why isn't God enough? I challenge you to really dig deep here and spend time wrestling with the answers.

As I shared in my story, I too longed to find my birth parents. But it wasn't until I decided God got to answer these questions, and He has the final say on my acceptance, that my life transformed. Did finding my birth parents bring me joy? The most! However, they did not define me. Was it interesting to learn more about my earthly creation? Yes! Of course it was. However, I know God planned my life. He created me. Despite learning about my birth parents, their stories, and getting to know them, that is all second to learning about God, His story, and getting to know Him.

I hope and pray you find peace around your origin story. God chose you for this path as a part of His plan for your life. Why? Only God knows. I pray He reveals it to you and that you can trust Him.

*~Wendy*

# ORDER INFORMATION

To order additional copies of this book, please visit
www.redemption-press.com.
Also available on Amazon.com and BarnesandNoble.com
or by calling toll-free 1-844-2REDEEM.

CPSIA information can be obtained
at www.ICGtesting.com
Printed in the USA
LVHW091039241120
672561LV00004B/322